Pro-Mo's
Secrets to Finding and Catching Walleyes

Book Written by Gary Roach, Randy Amenrud and Bob Jensen

Illustrated by Lee Melander, John Norlin and Charlie Dunemann

Cover Photo by Bob Jensen

Printing by Detroit Lakes Printing, Detroit Lakes, MN 56501

All Rights Reserved

Published by Pro-Mo's Secrets, Box 686, Sheffield, IA 50475

ISBN 0-9621233-1-5

Copyright Pro-Mo's Secrets, 1989

ABOUT THE COVER

Randy Amenrud gets ready to release a walleye he just took. We like to keep a few walleyes for the table every now and then, but we also practice selective release. In many bodies of water, it's best to keep the smaller ones for eating and let the bigger ones swim away. Once you learn the Secrets to Finding and Catching Walleyes, the lunkers will be on your line on a regular basis and you'll get used to letting the "walruses" go.

Table of Contents

Introduction —————————————— P.1

What is Pro-Mo's —————————————— P.7

1. Getting Ready —————————————— P.9

2. Sonar —————————————— P.13

3. Lake Lotsa' Walleyes —————————————— P.21

4. Lake Weed Walleyes —————————————— P.25

5. The Variables —————————————— P.29

6. Finding Them in the Spring —————————— P.47

7. Finding Them in the Summer —————————— P.57

8. Finding Them in the Fall ———————————— P.81

9. Rivers —————————————— P.91

10. Reservoirs —————————————— P.109

Introduction

The most basic concept of fishing is that you can't catch the fish unless you can find them. An angler can have all the best baits, rods, reels, boats, motors and electronics, but if you can't put the lure near the fish, you can't catch them. It's that simple. In this book, we hope to make it easier for you to find walleyes wherever and whenever you fish.

Walleyes, like most other fish, move around quite a bit throughout the year. They can be found in one area during the spring, another area in the summer, and an entirely different location in the fall. If an angler wants to consistently catch old marble eyes, it is important that the walleye's seasonal movements are understood.

Throughout the entire range of the walleye, there are a num-

ber of different types of lakes, rivers, and reservoirs that these glassy-eyed fish inhabit. Some of these bodies of water are deep and clear, some are shallow and muddy. Some lakes have a lot of points, sunken islands and reefs, some are featureless and weed-choked. There are rivers that are small and fast-moving, others are much larger and appear to be slower moving. Whatever the situation, the walleyes will usually be relating to something.

Walleyes don't always relate to structure. Most of the time they do, but in some cases they don't. Baitfish location can play a huge role regarding where the walleyes will be. Most of the time, however, the successful walleye angler will be fishing near some sort of irregularity in the lake bottom. The irregularity might be a small rise on the bottom, an area where bottom content changes from sand to rock, a turn in the weeds, an area where dirty water meets clearer water, or the spot where slack water meets some current. These areas will all hold fish from time to time.

You might not catch one quite as big as Roach's 13 plus pounder, but then again you've got a much better chance to do so if you know where to look for walleyes during the different seasons. Gary took this trophy at an In Fisherman Jamboree on a Fireball jig and 6 pound test XT line. Roach hasn't stopped grinning about this fish, one of the biggest walleyes taken in Minnesota in the last decade.

In this book we deal with the situations most frequently encountered by people who fish for walleyes. We also talk about some of the weird places where we've caught old marble eyes. The strange thing is, every time we've found walleyes in a place where we didn't expect them, there was a good reason for them being there.

When fishing for walleyes, or any specie of fish for that matter, it's a good idea to try to establish a pattern. Pattern fishing is nothing new, anglers have been doing it for years. Establishing a pattern is simply described as finding where the most walleyes are most susceptible to a bait. Let's say we pull onto a body of water and the first spot we try is a sunken island. We catch one small walleye. Next we move to an area where the water goes quickly from ten to fourteen feet, and we catch another small fish. Our next stop is a shoreline point, and on that point in twelve feet of water we take three quick fish, and they're all over two and a half pounds. We move to another point and take a few more nice fish in eleven to thirteen feet of water. You can bet we're going to continue working points, because that's where we've found the most active fish. Our pattern is fishing points in water eleven to thirteen feet deep.

Remember though, that patterns will change throughout the day. When the point fish slow down, work the general area around the point, then go back and try the spots where nothing was taken earlier, especially if you marked fish on your sonar. Frequently, some areas will be more productive at different times of the day.

Also remember that it takes three or four fish to make a good pattern. A group of fish will be in an area for a reason, but one fish will be in an area because it has to be somewhere.

We're going to cover walleye location very heavily in this book and make only general references to the methods for catching the fish in particular situations and locations. If you're interested in finding out the best types of lures to use in certain

Bill Preuss, left, and Tom Rosdail compare their catch. They teamed up with Gary Roach and jumped from rock pile to rock pile, taking the active fish and moving on. They returned to their spots every 45 minutes to an hour and usually popped two or three quick fish. Evidently they had their walleyes patterned.

situations, we suggest that you pick up a copy of our other books, Pro-Mo's Secrets to Jigging for Walleyes, and Pro-Mo's Secrets to Live-Bait Rigging for Walleyes.

It's important that we stress that there are frequently variables that will influence the walleye's location. Walleyes will be close to sunken islands in the summer, UNLESS the bait-fish are suspended over deep water. In that case, the walleyes might suspend over or under the baitfish. Another example. Incoming creeks and small rivers attract walleyes looking for a place to spawn in the spring, but usually aren't very good spots after that. UNLESS, as is the case in a good number of lakes, shiners move into the creek at night in the fall. If that happens, gold-sided fish

will follow the shiners into the creek in a big way. Be aware that to every general concept of finding walleyes there will be exceptions. THEY AREN'T ALWAYS WHERE YOU EXPECT THEM TO BE. The most important part of finding walleyes is dddto remain flexible. Don't sit on a spot all day just because you caught fish there yesterday, or last week, or last year. Fish move, and if you want to catch fish you will have to move too. Remember, you can't catch 'em if you can't find 'em. Be mobile, experiment, and before long you'll be Finding and Catching Walleyes wherever you might be fishing.

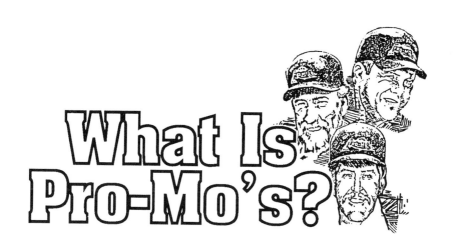

What Is Pro-Mo's?

Pro-Mo's is the shortened name of Fishing Pro-Mo's, a company dedicated to promoting fishing. We feel that fishing is a great individual or group activity, and we strive to make fishing a more enjoyable and productive experience for everyone who wants to try it by sharing our fish-catching secrets. Sure it's fun to go fishing and enjoy the outdoors, but it's a whole lot more fun to go fishing and catch some fish, whether they be walleyes, bass, panfish, or bullheads. Catchin' fish is fun, and we sincerely want you to catch more fish.

Pro-Mo's is made up of a group of individuals who are tournament anglers, guides, outdoor writers, seminar speakers, and just generally fishing educators. Pro-Mo's Team Members are top-notch anglers and good guys who enjoy sharing their fishing

Mark Roach, Pro-Mo's Team Member, used his knowledge of walleye habits to take this prize off a wind-blown point. When the wind blows, fat fish can be caught in thin water.

experiences and expertise with anyone who asks.

Pro-Mo's works with several manufacturers of fishing tackle in developing new products and refining already established fishing gear. The tackle makers that Pro-Mo's works with are equally committed to making fishing a more enjoyable and productive experience for everyone.

Next time you're on the water or in the parking lot of a tackle shop and see a boat with a Pro-Mo's decal, come on over and say hello. We'll be happy to tell you where we've been fishing and how we've been catching the fish. We want to share our angling information with you, and if you're onto a hot technique or lake, we would also like to hear about that. For now, though let's talk about Pro-Mo's Secrets to Finding and Catching Walleyes.

Chapter 1

*The First Step In
Finding Walleyes*

he first thing an angler should do when getting ready to chase walleyes is get a map of the body of water to be fished. The map will reveal the locations of incoming creeks, points, sunken islands, reefs, and other possible walleye holding areas. Remember, walleyes have areas that they are more likely to inhabit in the spring, different areas in the summer, and other structures in the fall. There are also some locations that the fish will use during more than one season. Nonetheless, having a general idea as to where the fish will be will help us eliminate large tracts of water before we even put the boat in.

Once the map has been studied, we should have a notion where we expect to start looking for marble eyes. It's still necessary though, to do some sonar work. No map is completely accurate.

It would have to be as big as the body of water being fished if it was to show every tiny sunken island and every detail. The map shows major structural elements, but it's up to the person fishing to find the smaller, unmarked structures. Often, the unmarked areas will be the most productive ones. Cruising an area with one eye on the depth-finder will not only help us in locating the areas marked on the map, it will aid in finding the unmarked spots.

In this book we are going to cover walleye location by season in lakes in the first section, rivers in the second and reser-

Whether it's professionally prepared or drawn by a fishin' buddy on the back of an envelope, a map will give an angler an idea of where to start to look for walleyes. Spend some time studying a map before you get on the lake and you'll cut down on time spent working unproductive water. All the better if you can get someone who has recently fished the lake to mark the map with tips for you.

voirs in the third.

We have created maps of bodies of water that have most of the main types of walleye structure. The particular body of water you fish may not have all the structural elements found in our lakes, but it will probably have a couple of the walleye attracting features contained in our lake map. Understanding how and when walleyes relate to certain areas is a major step in catching more gold-sided lunkers. Let's take a look at some maps and try to determine where we should concentrate our efforts in finding some walleyes that will be willing to "stretch our string".

Chapter 2

The Most Valuable Fishing Tool?

o find walleyes consistently throughout the year, an electronic sonar unit is an invaluable tool. When you understand how to interpret what your sonar is revealing, it
becomes possible to eliminate vast portions of unproductive water
and concentrate on the areas where most of the walleyes will be
found. It has been said that ten percent of the water holds ninety
percent of the fish. This is especially true with walleyes, as
they have a strong tendency to school. If we can find that ten
percent region of a body of water where most of the fish are,
we're well on our way to catching more fish. Sonar will help us
find that ten percent area much faster.

Sure, there are some instances when sonar isn't necessary to

find the fish, like when they're holding in slack water areas below dams or when they're jammed into the mouth of a creek in the spring. The wading angler doesn't rely on sonar equipment much either. By and large though, most walleye chasers who fish from boats will find that electronic sonar will help them catch more fish more regularly.

Jerry Smith on the left and Ron Hendrickson with a few of the walleyes they caught while fishing with Randy Amenrud. They were working a small point extending from a sunken island, and without sonar would have never found the spot. Jerry was on his first walleye trip. He quickly discovered that a walleye can't be lip-landed like he does with bass.

If you want that sonar to be an aid in catching walleyes, you must learn how to use it, then believe what it's telling you, and do what it tells you to do. If the unit shows that the fish are two feet

off the bottom in fifteen feet of water, and you're using a crankbait that only runs six feet below the surface, it might be a good idea to use a lure that will get down to the fish. The best

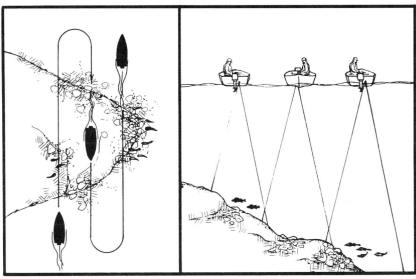

I-4. A top view of how we run a structure to determine which depth to start at. In this situation we have a point. We'll go across the point, keeping a close eye on the depth-finder, watching for fish activity to appear on the sonar. Go across the point and turn around and come back in water that's a little deeper. Again, watch for fish life on the sonar. Repeat this process several times or until you have a good idea of where the most fish activity is.

I-5. A bottom view of what we're trying to accomplish by running the structure. It's easy to see that some areas have fish, others don't. By going over a piece of structure several times, we can quickly locate the level with the most active fish. The cone coming from beneath the boat to the bottom is the cone angle of the sonar unit's transducer. With a twenty degree transducer, you'll usually be covering a bottom area about one third of the depth. For instance, if the water is fifteen feet deep, the area covered on the bottom will be about five feet in diameter. IMPORTANT: When running structure with an eye on the depth-finder, it's critical that you, or someone else in the boat is watching for other boats or obstructions in the water.

way to become familiar with your depth-finder is to get out on the water in areas you know and see what they look like on sonar. For instance, go to an area with a rocky bottom and see what rocks look like on the unit. Next go to an area with a sand bottom and see what it looks like. Next find some deep weeds. Pretty soon you'll be able to distinguish between rocks and fish that are close to the bottom. When you can do this, you're going to be much more proficient in catching walleyes.

There are a number of different types of sonar units available to anglers. We've used them all, and have found merit in most of them. For most walleye devotees though, a flasher, a LCG, and a paper graph are all completely adequate. We usually run a flasher alongside either a LCG or a paper graph. In fact, the old reliable flasher is still the sonar unit that gets turned on first in the morning and gets shut off last at the end of the day. These units will read well at top speed and give an accurate picture of what the bottom looks like.

It is important that the flasher being used is tuned to operate at it's optimum performance level. Too many anglers turn the unit on so the bottom depth is displayed, and don't bother to do any more tuning. Here's how we adjust our flashers so they show us all we need to know about the area being fished.

Many of the most popular flasher units have two controls, a sensitivity knob, and a suppressor knob. The sensitivity control is also the on\off switch. When the unit is turned on, there is a mark at zero, which indicates the power is on. Increase the sensitivity a little more, and a mark will appear at ten feet, for example. The water is this area is ten feet deep. Continue to increase the sensitivity until another mark appears at exactly double the bottom depth. If the water is ten feet deep, there should be another mark at twenty feet. This mark is called the second echo. The second echo indicates a hard bottom, probably sand, gravel,

or clay. If the sensitivity is turned all the way up and no second echo appears, the bottom content is soft, probably mud or silt. When the unit is displaying a second echo, the sensitivity setting is about right. Some anglers like to increase the sensitivity a lit-

An improperly tuned flasher on the left, a properly tuned flasher on the right. The water in this situation is fourteen feet deep. Note that the unit on the right has the sensitivity set high enough so the second echo, at twenty eight feet, is visible. Also, with the higher sensitivity setting, we note some baitfish near the surface and a larger fish close to the bottom. We choose Eagle and Lowrance electronics for all of our fishing. They're dependable, high-quality, and easy to use.

tle more, some prefer to back off a bit. Too much sensitivity will give a cluttered dial with lots of marks flashing all over, while too little sensitivity won't give a detailed picture of the bottom.

Keep the suppression setting as low as possible. Sometimes it's necessary to increase suppression to eliminate electric interference that can be caused by other sonar units or a high speed run, but never set the suppression any higher than necessary. Too much suppression will decrease sensitivity. If there is a walleye hovering close to the bottom, and if suppression is too high, the fish will blend in with the bottom signal. With the suppression

set correctly, fish just a few inches off the bottom should appear as a separate mark. Keep the sensitivity high enough to get a good second echo, and set the suppression no higher than necessary, and you'll get a good idea as to what the bottom looks like.

Generally, we use the flasher to find the spot to be fished. After the area has been located, we shut the flasher off and take a closer look at the area with a graph or LCG. These types of sonar draw a very detailed picture of the bottom and help us understand the exact location of the walleyes.

For the ultimate in detail, a high-quality paper graph can't be beat. The paper unit will separate fish just an inch or two from the bottom, and will also mark fish suspended in the weeds much better. If an exact picture of the bottom is important to you, a paper graph is just what you need. Sure it's necessary to replace graph paper every now and then, but that's a small price for the most detailed picture possible of the underwater world.

Several years ago, LCGs(Liquid Crystal Graphs) burst upon the scene. Some of the early units didn't draw that good a picture of the watery world, but they didn't require paper. In fact, there is nothing to replace with a LCG. In the past couple of years, the liquid crystals have been improved dramatically, and they are very simple to operate. A good liquid crystal will draw a picture that has almost as much detail as the paper unit, and they're generally more simple to operate. If you're in the market for your first sonar unit, or are looking for a graph-type unit to run in conjunction with a flasher, we recommend that you take a close look at the recent models of liquid crystal graphs.

As with flashers, run LCGs and paper graphs on the highest possible sensitivity setting. When the screen gets too cluttered or the paper has too many marks, back off on the sensitivity a little bit. Many graph units have an automatic setting that will set all the adjustments for you. Most units do an excellent job on auto

matic, but for the best picture possible, you will need to go to the manual mode. We suggest you become comfortable with the unit in the automatic mode before switching to manual.

LCGs and paper graphs have Grayline features that allow an angler to interpret whether the bottom is soft or hard, and whether those are fish or rocks tight to the bottom. They also have functions that allow a person to zoom in on a particular section of water. Let's say the water is thirty feet deep, but we want to look at only the bottom ten feet because that seems to be where the most fish activity is. Push the right buttons for the unit being used and a detailed blow-up of the bottom ten feet will appear on the screen or on the paper.

The new LCGs and paper graphs are incredible fish-finding tools. However, we still won't give up our flashers. Whether you choose to use a flasher, LCG, paper graph, or a combination of these units, learn to use them and believe what they're showing you. They will help you find and catch more walleyes.

Chapter 3

L ake Lotsa' Walleyes is a body of water that we've created. It exists only on paper, but it is very similar to many of the lakes that are found in walleye country. This body of water is an open system, which means that it has a creek or river coming in, and a creek or river going out. In this case the feeder creek is about midway in the lake on the north shore, while the draining creek is in the extreme southeast corner. The feeder can be as small as six to ten feet wide and only a couple of feet deep, or it can be thirty to fifty feet wide and ten feet deep. In Lake Lotsa' Walleyes the feeder is on the small side.

Our example lake is roughly 6,000 acres with a maximum depth of just over 100 feet. In addition to the feeder and outgoing

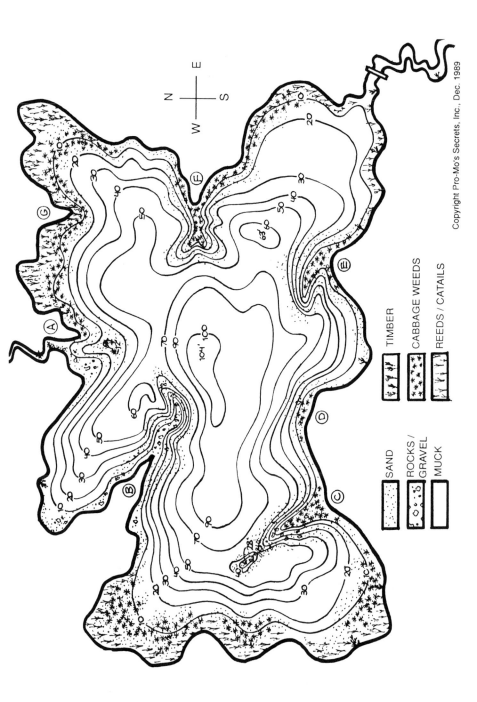

SAND ROCKS / GRAVEL MUCK

TIMBER CABBAGE WEEDS REEDS / CATAILS

Copyright Pro-Mo's Secrets, Inc., Dec. 1989

22

creek, there are points, sunken islands, drop-offs that go quickly and others that taper more gently, and also some shallow bays. This body of water has all the structural elements necessary to sustain a good population of naturally reproducing walleyes.

Water clarity is pretty good. On a clear day the bottom can be seen in five or six feet of water. There's plenty of food for the walleyes to eat. Perch can be found on the weedlines, points, and sunken islands, with cisco and tullibee being found in the open water areas, and lake shiners inhabit the shallower, sandy areas. There is also a mayfly hatch.

The walleyes share this lake with some other predators. There is a developing population of largemouth bass that can be found in the vegetation in the shallow bays and along the weedlines, and some trophy northern pike cruise the deep weedlines.

There are also good numbers of crappies, sunfish, and bluegills. However, walleye populations are the strongest. In general, life is good for the walleyes that call Lake Lotsa' Walleyes home.

Chapter 4

L ake Weed Walleye is another body of water that we've created because there's a whole bunch of lakes of this type out there, and many of the lakes like this have lots of glassy-eyed fish.

This lake is a closed system. There is no feeder creek, and no draining creek. Some natural reproduction of walleyes occurs here, but stocking is necessary to sustain good populations of walleyes. Some state fish agencies won't stock a lake of this type unless there is a public boat ramp.

Lake Weed Walleye has limited fish attracting structure. There are a couple of shallow sunken islands, one major point, a couple of minor points, and some scattered rock and grav-

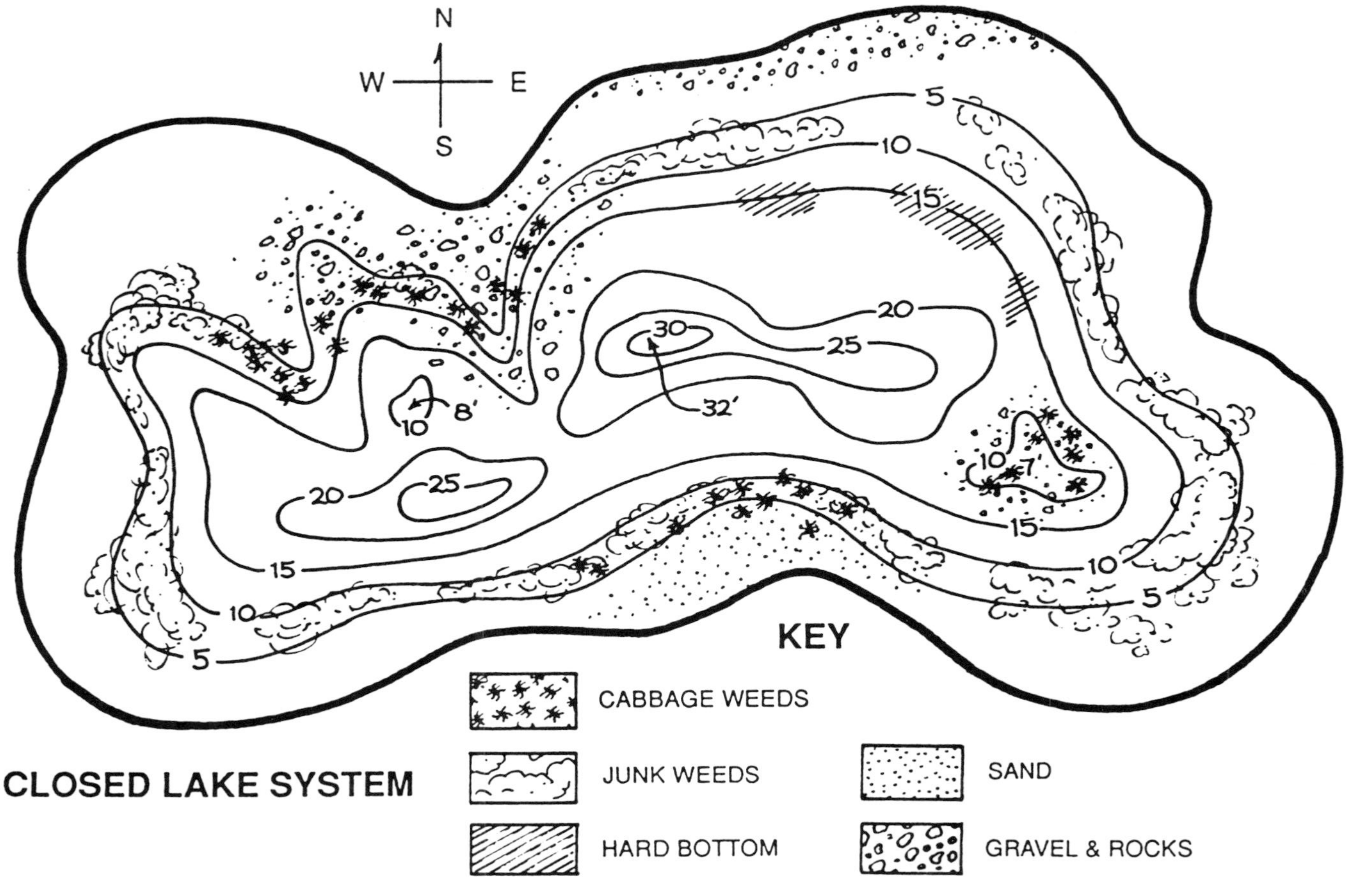

CLOSED LAKE SYSTEM

KEY

CABBAGE WEEDS

JUNK WEEDS

HARD BOTTOM

SAND

GRAVEL & ROCKS

26

el. There is also a lot of vegetation, including cabbage weed. This lake covers about six hundred acres , although lakes of this type will range from fifty to over a thousand acres in size.

The maximum depth of this body of water is just over thirty feet, and bottom can be viewed in water two to three feet deep. The walleyes feed on a mixed diet of perch, minnows, even panfish and bullheads from time to time. Other major gamefish include a strong population of largemouth bass and some northern pike, although the majority of the pike don't get very big.

Chapter 5

How They Affect Walleye Location

t seems like the only thing we can count on when fishing walleyes is that things are going to change. The wind can switch directions and intensity, water clarity can get better or worse, a bright day can become overcast, and who knows what else might happen. All these factors can have an influence on where the walleyes are going to be, and if we're going to consistently catch fish, we must take into consideration how the walleyes are going to react under the different conditions.

Knowing how the fish usually react to a certain condition is no guarantee that they'll always react that way. In some bodies of water, and even in some particular areas of that body of water, the fish will, at times, react differently than expected. We'll fill you in on the "unexpected" reactions that we're familiar with, but

keep in mind that when on the water, it's best to determine where to fish based on how the walleyes usually react to a condition. For example, walleyes usually are most active on the wind-blown side of a reef, but there are conditions when they'll be found on the down-wind side of that reef. Not very often, but sometimes. We'll talk about that later. For now, let's discuss the variables that will help in determining walleye location.

LIGHT-PENETRATION

Light penetration has a major impact concerning where the walleyes will be. Some of the other variables we'll talk about are of prime importance because they have a large effect on light penetration. For our use, we describe light penetration simply as the amount of light that's getting into a particular area. Light penetration changes from one walleye structure to another, from hour to hour, and very definitely from one lake to another. Water clarity and wind action will influence how much light will penetrate to a particular depth, as will the season of the year and the shape of the structure. We'll talk about all of these factors in this chapter. Let's talk about how water clarity affects light penetration first.

WATER CLARITY

Water clarity has a tremendous effect on light penetration and walleye location, and the consistent walleye catcher will consider water clarity when looking for an area where the fish will most likely be found. Once we understand how water clarity influences walleye activity and location, we'll be one step closer to catching old marble eyes on a more regular basis. Water clarity affects how far light can penetrate. Obviously, the darker the water, the less light penetration there will be. Light can

penetrate farther in clear water than dirty, so it will be brighter on the bottom in ten feet of clear water than it will be in ten feet of dirty water. The fish will have better vision in clear water, but this doesn't necessarily mean fishing will be better in clear water.

Anglers have different definitions of water clarity. Water that one fisher-person would consider to be clear might be seen as dirty water to another angler. We have a guideline that we use when deciding on water clarity. If bottom can't be seen in water depths deeper than two feet, the water is dirty. If the bottom is visible in water deeper than two feet but less than six, stained water conditions have been encountered. If the bottom can be viewed deeper than six feet, consider the water to be clear.

Now that we've got a guideline to help determine water clarity, how do we apply that to finding gold-sided fish. First, water clarity can help us decide which lake we should try. Water with some color warms more quickly than clear water, so often-times in the spring the walleyes will become active in the dirty water lakes first. If the walleyes in a body of water are feeding heavily before the spawn, they'll be easy to catch. At the same time, a clearer body of water just down the road will be several degrees cooler and the fish will still be somewhat lethargic. Spend your time catching the easy fish in the body of water that has more color.

Eventually, the fish in the dirty body of water will begin spawning and feeding activity will slow down. At about the same time, the water in the clear water lake will be warm enough for the walleyes to start becoming active. Now you should be chasing those fish. When the clear water walleyes start spawning, the walleyes in the dirty water lake should be finished with the reproduction ritual and ready to start feeding again. Jump back to that body of water and you'll stay on top of the most active fish.

That's how we use water clarity to determine which body of

water to fish in. Here's how we use water clarity to decide where to start looking for walleyes once we've decided which body of water we should be fishing.

Typically, dirty water fish will be found much shallower than walleyes in clear water. At times the walleyes in dirty water can be found deep, but most of the time we would expect to find them in water from two to twelve feet deep.

Dirty water walleyes will also hold tightly to structure. When working a rock-pile, drop-off, or weed-bed, don't wander too far away from that fish-holding area. If the walleyes are using that piece of structure, they'll be close to it. Walleyes in dirty or stained will hold much tighter to structure than their relatives in clear water.

Walleyes in dirty or stained water will frequently be more active under bright conditions than walleyes in clear water. That's why bodies of water with murky water will outproduce systems with clear water on bright days. The color in the water reduces light penetration, which seems to encourage the fish to remain active throughout the day. In lakes with clear water, the fish are usually more active on overcast days and at dawn and dusk, as well as at night.

When working a body of water that's clear, especially on a bright day, it pays to search out areas that might have cloudier water. In lakes with a feeder stream, the area around the incoming feeder might be cloudier, especially if that stream is swollen with run-off from a recent rain or snow-melt. The surrounding water is clear, but the water that the creek is bringing in is stained or dirty. The murkier water will often hold walleyes, and those fish will frequently be feeding.

Mudlines are a common occurrence on many reservoirs. If the wind has been beating into a shoreline that has lots of clay or sand, much of that sand and clay will be washed into the water.

This creates a very definite line where the dirty water meets the clearer section. This dirty water will often attract the walleyes just like the stained water that the feeder stream we just talked about will.

Give a lot of consideration to water clarity when selecting a lake to chase walleyes on. Some of the clear water systems have excellent populations of walleyes, but they can be a monster to fish. We usually like to see a little color in the water, and sometimes a lot of color is a good deal. There are also a couple of other variables that will play a role in how important water clarity is. A good rule of thumb however, is to select a lake with dingier water on bright days, and save the clear water lakes for overcast days, night-fishing, and periods of low-light penetration.

WIND

Wind also has an effect on light penetration. The wind creates waves, and waves cut down on light penetration. That's why you'll find walleyes on a shallow reef on a bright day if it's windy. Take the same reef on a bright, calm day, and frequently it will be devoid of fish.

We generally start looking for walleyes on the wind-blown side of the lake, and the wind-blown side of a structure. Walleyes will usually be most active on the side of the lake or reservoir that the wind is blowing into because that's where light penetration is reduced. Same's true for a piece of structure, and also, baitfish may be disoriented on the side of a structure that's catching the wind due to the waves. However, keep in mind that a good walleye structure that is not windblown will still be better than a poor walleye area that is windblown. Walleyes are opportunistic fish and will go where the eatin's easiest.

We are aware of one situation in which the fish will be active on the downwind side of a structure. Let's say we have a shallow reef that runs parallel to shore, which is about 200 yards away. The wind is blowing hard across the reef toward shore. The waves are crashing into the shore, then washing back into the lake. Remember, the waves are coming all the way across the body of water, collecting water as they go. When they hit the shore, they start to go back toward the main body of water. This causes a back current or undertow. The waves are blowing toward shore when they come over the reef, but after they hit the shore the water runs back toward the reef. Walleyes will position themselves on the side of the reef that faces shore in this situation.

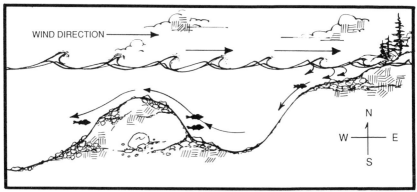

Usually the walleyes will be on the side of the structure that the wind is blowing into. Here's an exception. The wind is blowing from the west over a shallow hump that is anywhere from 100 yards to a half-mile off the east shoreline. The current on the surface is coming into the shoreline, but all that water crashing into the shoreline has to go somewhere, creating a reverse current below the surface. The water that hits the shoreline is actually flowing back into the lake. In this situation, many of the walleyes will be on the down-wind side of the hump. If this structure were farther from the shoreline, the reverse current would probably not be noticeable and the walleyes would be on the side of the hump that the wind was blowing into.

Most of the time though, look for the active fish to be in the wind-blown areas.

There are some wind directions that we prefer over others. It

seems that north, northeast, and northwest winds can have a detrimental effect on fishing success. They usually indicate a coming change in weather. Winds from the northwest usually bring Arctic air with them, and that means colder conditions which can shut the fish off, especially in the spring and fall.

Winds from the south or southwest are frequently good fishing winds. They bring warmer air, which can be a good deal in the spring and fall. They also commonly indicate stable weather conditions.

Consider wind direction, but don't stay home just because the wind is blowing from the northwest. We've taken lots of fish when a northerner was blowing. Fishing might not be as good as it could be, but any time spent on the water should be a learning experience, and that's another step in the direction of more consistent fishing success.

TIME OF YEAR

A factor that many anglers don't consider when light penetration is being considered is that the time of year has a bearing on how deep the light will penetrate. In the spring and fall, the days are shorter and the sun is lower in the sky. In the summer, the days are longer and the sun is more directly overhead. The sun's rays are much more direct in the summer, therefore, light penetration is much greater. In the spring and fall, the sun's rays are at more of an angle, so light penetration is reduced.

How does this factor influence fish location? It simply means that if all else is equal, the walleyes can, from time to time, be found shallower in the spring and fall in some lakes than they might be in the summer. On a calm, clear day in the fall, the fish may be using water shallower than they would on a calm, clear day in the middle of the summer. Remember though, the term shallow is relative. In some bodies of water, the walleyes might be in forty feet of water in the summer and move up into the twenty foot depths in the fall. In other walleye puddles, the fish might be in ten foot areas in the summer and move into three and four foot depths under the same conditions in the fall or spring when the sun's rays angles are less.

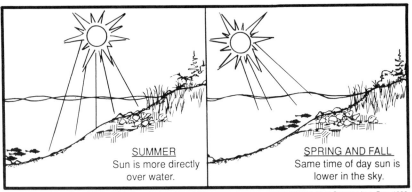

I-8. The position of the sun in the sky makes a difference as to where the fish will be. In the spring and fall the sun is lower in the sky and it's rays don't penetrate as far. The fish will frequently be shallower.

In the summer the sun is more directly overhead, it's rays penetrate deeper, and the fish will usually be found in deeper water. Remember though, that cloud cover and wave action will also have an effect on how deep the sun's rays will penetrate.

SHAPE OF STRUCTURE

The physical shape of the structure will have a bearing on how much light penetration there is in a particular area. First off, let's talk about how actual structure configuration will affect light penetration, then how the fish will react.

Let's say we have a sunken island in the middle of a body of water. This island is flat on the top, comes within ten feet of the surface, and is surrounded by twenty two feet of water on all sides. The degree of taper is the same all the way around the island. On

overcast days and at night, the light penetration is the same all the way around the island. During the day though, some areas of this piece of structure will see more light penetration at times, some areas will receive less light penetration at certain times of the day.

Before the sun peeks over the horizon at dawn, all parts of the sunken island will have about the same amount of light penetra-

Jim McDonnell caught this fish on a bright, calm day by fishing the shaded side of a sunken island with a Roach Rig and inflated crawler. Mac is a guide on some of the midwest's toughest water and consistently puts his clients on lots of walleyes.

tion, which will be very little. However, after the sun comes up in the east, the east side of the island will be bathed in light, while the west side of the island will still have limited light penetration. The taper of the drop-off along the west side of the structure will provide shade, and light penetration will be minimal.

In the morning the west side of the structure will be shaded. Expect to find the easiest-to-catch walleyes to be on the west side in the shade.

At mid-day when the sun is directly overhead, there is very little shade anywhere on the structure. The fish can be almost anywhere.

Later in the afternoon as the sun sinks in the western sky, the east side of the structure will be shaded. That's where many of the walleyes will be found.

As the sun gets higher in the sky, more of the island will be exposed to the effects of the sun's rays. When the sun gets to the point where it's directly over the island, light penetration will be almost the same for the entire structure. As the sun continues it's daily trek across the sky, the west side of the island will be more exposed to it's rays, the east side will start to be shaded. Light penetration will be greater on the west side, less on the east side.

How will the walleyes react to the different sun positions on this particular piece of structure? Light penetration will have a big influence on where the most active fish will be. On an overcast day they could be active on any side of the sunken island. On a bright day however, the position of the sun will play a large role in determining where the most easy-to-catch walleyes will be. In the morning as the sun is rising, the east side of the sunken structure will be bathed in sunlight. This can, and frequently will cause the walleyes to be less aggressive and tougher to catch. On the west side of the island however, light penetration will be much less due to the shade provided by the side of the island. The fish will be much more aggressive on this side of the structure now.

As the sun gets higher in the sky, light penetration will be greater everywhere on the sunken island. The fish could drop deeper, or they could shut off. We have seen times when the walleyes went on a good bite when the sun got high in the sky and there was no wind, but most of the time they'll be most easily caught in deeper water when the sun is high.

Later in the afternoon the west side of the island will be most exposed to the sun and the east side will start to see light penetration decrease. As light penetration increases on the west side, the fish will be less active, while the walleyes on the east side will start feeding again. If you want to continue to catch fish, move back to the east side of the island, start working the deep water areas and move shallower as the sun gets lower in the sky. When the sun hits a certain point in the sky, the walleyes on the west side will start biting again. This certain point varies from lake to lake, and only time on the water will tell exactly at what point those fish will start biting again.

Remember, the sunken island we just talked about had the same degree of taper all the way around it. The drop-off was the same all the way around the island. Most structures have irregular drops. In one area the break will be fast, in other areas the break will be much slower. The degree of taper will also have an effect on the amount of light penetration.

Let's pretend we're on a lake with two sunken islands. Both islands top out at eight feet and are surrounded by twenty eight feet of water. The only difference is that on the west side of one island the depth tapers gradually to the twenty eight foot depth, while on the other structure the drop-off is much faster. On the island with the slow taper it's at least fifty yards from the top of the island to the twenty eight foot depth. On the other structure,

move the boat twenty feet off the shallow part of the island and you'll be over the deep water. This difference in taper of the drop-off will have a big effect on light penetration, and light penetration, as we've discussed, will have a big effect on the walleye's behavior.

The difference in the degree of taper of the drop-off will determine how soon the base of the drop-off receives increased light penetration. When the drop-off is gradual, the deep water receives increased light penetration much sooner in the day than on a drop-off that is fast. On the fast breaking island, the side of the structure acts almost like an umbrella that is shading the deep water along the side of the island.

How does the difference in degree of taper affect the walleyes? Remember that we're working the west side of each island. As the sun gets higher in the sky in the morning, the slow tapering structure is flooded with light and the fish will slow down or shut off. On the fast tapering area, the light penetration will remain low and the fish will continue to feed. When the fish stop hitting on the slow tapering area, head to the fast tapering area for continued action.

There are times when a fast tapering area is receiving as much light penetration as a slow tapering location, such as when the sun is directly overhead. However, those periods are generally shorter. If a slow tapering area is getting lots of light penetration for five hours, the fast taper might get the same amount of light for only three hours.

Just because a fast breaking area is shielded from the sun doesn't mean it will always be the best spot. There are times when the walleyes seem to prefer a slow breaking area. However, when the light penetration is high, although there may be more walleyes on the slow tapering area, they could be tougher to catch. Although there are fewer fish on the fast taper, they

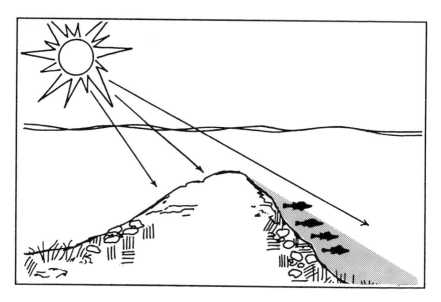

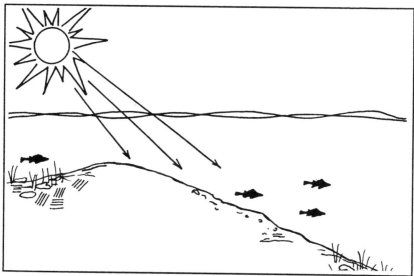

Here we have two sunken islands. They both rise to about ten feet from the surface. The difference is, the island in the top illustration drops off quickly on the right side while the island in the bottom illustration has a more gradual taper. The fast tapering side of the island provides some shade, while the gradual tapering island doesn't. Frequently, the walleyes will gather and remain inactive in the shaded area of the structure. As the sun gets more directly overhead, the shaded area will get smaller until it too is exposed to the sun's rays.

might be more willing to take a bait. This is when walleye fishing comes down to a game of odds. Always fish the spots where the most active fish will be and you'll end up catching more walleyes.

WEATHER CONDITIONS

Weather conditions can play a big part in fishing success. Some weather conditions create good fishing conditions, some create fair conditions, and some weather just plain makes for poor action. However, we suggest that you go fishing whenever you can, regardless of weather conditions, at least to a limit. Obviously you should get off the water during an electrical storm or during dangerous winds. Don't stay home though just because conditions aren't ideal for catching fish. If you wait for ideal conditions, you might not get to go fishing very much in the course of a year.

Stable weather conditions are what we like to see for the best action. Three, four, or five days in a row when conditions stay the same make walleyes the most patternable and easiest to catch. In the spring and fall, a few warm days in a row will create a good angling opportunity. Stable weather and wind blowing from a consistent direction in the summer will put the walleyes on the bite. Stability makes for good fishing.

As many fishermen know, the scourge of good fishing is a cold front. It's a good thing we have cold fronts or many of us would have to look for a new excuse for not catching anything. Actually, cold fronts aren't the blame for poor action, it's the post-frontal conditions. Here's a common scenario. We're on the water about seven o'clock at night. It's hot and humid, with little breeze. Off in the distance we notice storm clouds building, and we may even hear a little thunder. We know it's going to storm, but we don't care because the walleyes are really going. We're catching them shallow and deep, over rocks and in the cabbage. They're hitting jigs, crankbaits, live-bait rigs, and anything else we might throw at them. It's some of the best action we've ever had. This action is taking place during prefrontal conditions, which are frequently good for fishing.

That night while we're sleeping, the front goes through. It rains and lightnings and thunders. The next morning we walk outside to a bright, crisp, clear day. The air temperature's dropped twenty degrees and there's not a cloud in the sky. We're now experiencing the post-frontal conditions, and you can bet that fishing is going to be a lot tougher than it was last night. Last night the walleyes were everywhere, today they're going to be much tougher to find, and even more dificult to catch. The fish might be schooled tightly on a small piece of structure like the tip of a point, or, if the body of water being fished has little in the way of structure, the fish will scatter. There'll be one here, another one there, but no real strong concentrations. If you're on a lake that has a good deal of structure and you pop a fish under post-frontal conditions, work that specific spot and maybe you'll take another walleye or two. On an under-structured lake, work the general area where the fish was caught but don't sit on one particular spot. Keep an eye on your sonar and let it tell you if the fish are schooled or scattered.

We feel that post-frontal conditions have a more harmful effect on fishing success in the spring and fall. Remember, two of the weather characteristics that accompany post-frontal conditions are clear skies and a decrease in temperatures. In the spring and fall the decrease in temperatures can have a dramatic effect on the walleye's activity level, while the decrease in the summer have a minimal effect.

Let's say we're fishing a body of water in the spring or fall. The water has been, let's say, fifty degrees for several days, and

the fish have been active. Fifty degree water temps are a level at which walleyes will be active. A cold front goes through and the post-frontal conditions linger for several days. The water temps fall seven degrees to forty three degrees and the fish shut off. Walleyes will feed if the water temperature is forty three and rising, but if the water temp was considerably higher and falls to forty three, fishing success will suffer.

Now let's look at the same conditions in the summer. Water temps are seventy eight degrees on the surface. A front goes through and temperatures go down to seventy one degrees. That's still well within a walleye's temperature range where it will remain active. Fishing action will decline, but probably not because of the decline in water temperature.

What then causes action to taper off after the passage of a cold front in the summer? Light penetration is our choice for the culprit. Clear, bright skies are synonymous with post-frontal conditions, and the clear, bright skies have more to do with the feeding habits of walleyes in the summer than a moderate decline in temperatures. The sun is directly overhead in the summer, and with no cloud cover to filter out the sun's rays, the fish need to find areas of more shade. Also, the passage of the front seems to cleanse the atmosphere. Have you ever noticed how crisp and clean the air seems after a front has gone through? Perhaps this cleansing effect allows the sun's rays to penetrate farther into the water, making the walleyes even more susceptible to the increased light penetration.

Whatever the case, we've found that in the spring and fall a decrease in water temperature will give walleyes lockjaw. If post-frontal conditions are encountered during either of these seasons, search out the warmest water you can find. This is where the walleyes will be most active and easiest to catch.

In the summer, look for areas of shade. If a weedline is being worked, expect the most action to occur on the shaded side of the weeds. Same's true for sunken islands and points. The shaded areas will be the best. Action could get better late in the day as the sun starts to go down, especially if the water has been warming all day.

Don't stay home just because a cold front has gone through. Fish the warmest water available in the spring and fall, and work the shaded areas in the summer, and you should get at least get the landing net wet a few times.

Chapter 6

Walleyes in Lakes

Finding Them in the Spring

First Trip Fever

Fishing fever bites most of us early in the year and we get on the water as soon as possible. In some states, there is no closed season on walleyes and it's possible to get out there as soon as the ice goes out. In other regions we have to wait until season opens. Regardless of where we fish in the spring, the walleyes will more than likely be in some stage of their annual spawning ritual. They'll either be getting ready to spawn, actually spawning, or just finishing. Walleyes will seek out particular areas of the lake in which to lay their eggs, and they'll be in these areas for perhaps a week or ten days prior to the spawn, and for a few days after.

Most states set their fishing seasons to protect the spawning fish, so most openers will fall after the walleyes have gone

through the reproductive process. In states where spawning fish aren't protected, we feel that it's important that anglers don't get greedy. Walleyes that are getting ready to spawn can be very susceptible to a jig and minnow, and it's possible to take a bunch of fish. There's nothing wrong with keeping a few of the smaller male fish for supper, but don't fill the freezer just because fishin's easy. Release the females so they can complete the process of repopulating their species.

On our maiden fishing trip of the season, the first place we will look for likely walleye holding areas is on the north shore of the lake. The water on the north side warms up quicker because it receives the full brunt of the sun's rays, and at this time of year, the most active fish will be in the areas with the warmer water. Water temperatures will frequently be several degrees warmer on the north side than the south side, so that's where we'll expect to find the most active walleyes.

We pay the most attention to water temperatures early in the year. Water temperature can be important during the other seasons, but we feel they're most important in fish location and the activity level of the walleyes in the spring.

Walleyes in different bodies of water will spawn at different water temperatures. We've seen them in the spawn in water that was 38 degrees, and we've also seen them spawning in 48 degree temps. That's quite a variance. Spawning temps vary from lake to lake, and even from fish to fish in some instances. In some bodies of water you'll find walleyes spawning in 40 degree temps, while other fish in the same lake or river will spawn in 46 degree water. We don't know for sure why it happens this way, but we assume it's nature's way of making sure things will work out for the best in terms of a successful walleye spawn.

By considering water temperatures, we can stay on the most active walleyes for a longer period of time. Remember, fish are

cold-blooded creatures, and their activity levels are affected by water temperatures. The warmer the water gets, the more active the fish get, to a certain extent. Abnormally warm water will cause a decrease in activity, but that's not a consideration in the spring. As water temps increase in the spring, the fish become more and more active until they actually begin spawning. When they begin spawning, the urge to feed diminishes. Now is the time to move to a different area of the lake and look for more active fish.

Let's say we've been fishing one particular area for several days. The water temp has been 44 degrees in that area and the fish have been easy to catch. Now the water temp has risen to 47 degrees and the fish begin spawning. The larger females become tough to catch, although the smaller male fish will still take a bait. Start looking in different areas of the lake for potential spawning areas where the water temp is in the 44 degree range. It could be that there are active walleyes there that haven't started the egg-laying ritual yet, and they could be biters. By considering water temperatures and moving around, it's possible to stay on active, easy to catch walleyes much longer.

As mentioned, we're going to begin our search for walleyes on the north shore. The prime spot that immediately jumps off the map of Lake Lotsa' Walleyes is the incoming creek. Walleyes are by nature fish of the river, and the current that the creek provides will attract large numbers of glassy-eyed fish. The stronger the current, the more fish creeks will pull in.

The addition of a pea gravel bottom will enhance this spot. Bottom composition has a big influence as to how many walleyes will use an area during the spawn. Pea gravel, rocks, and sand are the preferred spawning locations when available.

Typically, the walleyes will move up into the creek at night. They will also venture into the moving water on a cloudy day, and, if the water coming from the creek into the lake is dirty, the fish could be up in that stained water most of the time. In fact, if there isn't a lot of boat traffic to spook the walleyes, they could be in the creek even if the water and sky were clear. Generally though, the cloudier the sky and the more stained the water, the more the fish will use the creek.

How far up the creek the fish will go is dependent on how deep and how big the feeder is. A large, deep creek or river will attract more walleyes than a small, shallow stream. A feeder that has just a couple feet of water will have walleyes visit during low-light conditions, but the fish will pull out when the sun starts to come up or the skies clear. A deeper river will have fish in it all the time. The fish will move shallow at night, and drop into holes in the river during the bright part of the day.

Mike Howard and Chuck Brunner with a catch of spring walleyes. These fish were taken on sixteenth and eighth ounce Lipstick and Foxee jigs on a shallow point. Chuck caught more, but Mike took the biggest one.

If the walleyes do move out of the creek during the day, they will probably move back to the first drop-off. Look for an area near the creek where the depth drops quickly and you'll probably find the holding area for the walleyes when they aren't in the creek.

The walleyes using the creek area as a spawning ground will be the first to begin egg-laying. The water that the creek is bringing into the lake will be warmer, which will cause the fish to start spawning earlier than anywhere else. When the fish start spawning, the action will die off and it's time to look for a new spot.

The next most productive area will probably be the large point just west of the feeder creek. This point has a shallow area that is gravel-strewn, and there is deeper water nearby. It is also in a location that should be wind-blown, and wind-blown areas are almost as appealing to the walleyes as areas of current.

The walleyes will behave on the point almost like they did in the creek. They'll move shallow when light conditions are low, and move back to the drop-off when light increases. The only difference is, they'll use this point year'round.

Remember, how water temperature affects the walleyes? When the fish on this point start spawning, they'll get tougher to catch. Now we'll move to the point on the east shore. Maybe the fish there will be right for catching. The two points on the south shore will be the last places we check. All of these areas will hold fish this time of year, but the spots that we checked first on the north shore will probably hold the most fish, and will be the scene of the most active fish early in the season. Keep in mind that all the walleyes in the lake won't be doing the same thing at the same time. Some will be getting ready to spawn, some will actually be spawning, and others will be finished with egg-laying. Our task is to find the fish that are the easiest to catch. When the fish near the creek are getting ready to spawn, they'll be the easiest to catch, but when they start spawning, the fish on the north shore point will be more susceptible to being caught. When those fish begin egg-laying, we'll move to another point. When the fish on the south shore points are spawning, the walleyes that spawned near the creek will be recovered from the reproduction ritual and might be ready to start feeding ravenously. Water temperatures in the different areas of the lake will vary, and the walleyes feeding moods will vary accordingly. By finding the areas where the walleyes are feeding most actively, you're increasing the chances of catching more fish.

These fish can be caught using a variety of techniques, but the best producer most of the time will be a jig and minnow combination. However, live-bait rigs, slip-bobbers, and minnow-imitating baits will also catch them.

If we suspected the walleyes were spread out in the shallows of the spawning areas, we would try several approaches. First, we might try long-line trolling minnow imitating crankbaits. Try different sizes and colors until the productive one is found, and be sure to let plenty of line out. The boat passing overhead will spook the fish and they usually won't hit a lure close to the boat. Sixty or seventy feet is usually far enough back, but if the walleyes are skittish, you may need to let more line out. You can also try long-lining live-bait rigs when the walleyes are shallow. This approach will work day or night, but is usually better at night.

When the walleyes drop into the deeper holding areas as they so often do during the day, we like to back-troll with a jig and minnow or a live-bait rig and minnow. If the fish don't want a minnow, try a leech or crawler. We like fatheads or shiners about three inches long. Cover the different depths near the spawning area, and experiment with jig size and color. We usually find an eighth ounce jig to be about the right size, and chartreuse,

pink/white, and black have all been good colors. Try all the color combinations until you find what works best.

If you have the fish pin-pointed, it works best to cast to them, especially if they're shallow. By staying away and casting, you cut down on the possibility of spooking them. Again, we like to cast jigs, but crankbaits, slip-bobber rigs, and even live-bait rigs will be effective when casting to shallow walleyes. The most common place to cast to the walleyes this time of the year will be when they're in the mouth of the creek or on the shallow part of the points.

SPRING WALLEYE LOCATION IN LAKE WEED WALLEYE

Remember when we spoke about water temperatures having an affect on the activity level of the walleyes? We moved from area to area of Lake Lotsa' Walleyes as the water temps changed in hopes of staying on the most active fish. We can also accomplish this task of staying on the most active walleyes by moving from lake to lake. Lake Weed Walleye has fewer surface acres and is shallower than Lake Lotsa' Walleyes, so it warms up faster in the spring than Lake Lotsa' Walleyes. Therefore, the walleyes in this smaller body of water will also become active sooner. In fact, we might even select this type of lake as being a good choice to open on. In this body of water, the walleyes might be up shallow and feeding while the fish in Lake Lotsa' Walleyes are still sluggish. When the walleyes in this shallow puddle shut off during their attempted spawning ritual, the fish in Lake Lotsa' Walleyes should be up and prime for catching. When those fish start spawning, move back to the shallower, weedier lake. By now those walleyes should be done with spawning and ready to start feeding again. By considering water temps and understanding how they influence the fishes' activities, it's much easier to stay on top of the most active and easy to catch walleyes.

Finding the walleyes in the spring in Lake Weed Walleye is not difficult. Start looking for them on the north shore just like we did on Lake Lotsa' Walleyes. That's where the water will warm up first, so that's where the first active fish will appear. There's no incoming creek to attract the fish, but if there was, that's where we would start looking. On Lake Weed Walleye, the best areas for walleyes in the spring would be the shallow, hard bottom areas. The best looking spot on the map is the point extending out from the north shore. The large, shallow shelf covered with rocks and gravel will attract the most walleyes, and the quick access to deeper water is also attractive. At this time of the year, the walleyes will be scattered across this point, and will be found in water from two to seven feet deep much of the time.

The scattered rock humps all along the north shore east of the major point will also hold walleyes. There will be fish scattered on that shoreline out to about ten feet, but the largest concentrations of walleyes will be on the rocks. Although depth doesn't change much, the change in bottom make-up, from sand and gravel to rocks, seems to really attract and hold old marble-eyes. If you can find small rock humps surrounded by sand or gravel this time of year in the shallows, they can be a top-producing area.

In small lakes, the difference in water temperatures might not be very much from the south shore to the north shore. We still expect the warmest water to be on the north side most of the time in the spring, but the difference just might not be very much. Be sure to check out the south shore of Lake Weed Walleyes for scattered rock humps. There will be fish on the sand shoreline on the south side of the lake, but again, they'll be grouped much tighter on the rocky humps.

Generally, the two sunken islands in the middle of the lake

won't be very productive early in the year. Later on in the summer and fall they'll hold fish, but not yet. Early in the year, the most active walleyes will be relating to shallower shore structure on most types of lakes.

Another area that will hold spring walleyes in a lake of this type is newly emergent vegetation. Sand grass and cabbage that has just started growing will both attract gold fish. Grass no more than eight to twelve inches tall will draw and hold walleyes. Sometimes the fish will nestle into the weeds and lay flat on the bottom, other times they'll hover just over the top of the vegetation.

Copyright Pro-Mo's Secrets, Inc., Dec. 1989

A common situation in many lakes during the spring. The shallow hump has sand grass that is surrounded by cabbage weeds. The walleyes lurk on the edge of the cabbage during bright conditions, then move into the open areas to feed when the light decreases.

One of the best situations for finding fish in the short grass is when the short grass is surrounded by taller vegetation. One of the best conditions for this pattern is when taller cabbage surrounds a pocket of shorter sandgrass on a shallow hump. The shallowest portion of the hump is covered with short sandgrass, and that area is surrounded by the taller cabbage. Walleyes will hold on the shaded fringe where the short grass meets the taller cabbage. On overcast days the fish will move up into the shorter grass, but on bright days they'll hold on the shaded fringe section. This is a fairly common pattern, but one that many anglers overlook.

Lure selection and presentation on Lake Weed Walleye will be about about the same as on Lake Lotsa' Walleyes. Jigs, rigs, and minnow imitating baits will all produce. Use these lures in the spots we just talked about and you will catch walleyes.

Chapter 7

Walleyes in Lakes

Finding Them in the Summer

Which Way Did They Go?

S ummer, to many people, is vacation time, and lots of folks like to spend their vacation on the water chasing walleyes. When weather conditions are stable, walleye location frequently won't change a lot from day to day in the summer. The schools of fish will move around or up and down some, but if you found the walleyes on a big sunken island yesterday, and if weather conditions have remained the same, and if you didn't tell everyone within shouting distance where the fish were, they will probably still be in that same general vicinity today. This is especially true with walleyes that are in the deeper water areas. They'll hold within a certain area for several days at a time, and if their food base doesn't move and their surroundings remain stable, they might hang around longer.

In our two sample lakes, the location of the walleyes in the spring was about the same. They were in the shallows relating to hard bottom areas. In the summer, things change. The gold- sided fish are going to be relating to distinctly different areas in the two different bodies of water. You'll have some walleyes in similar locations in the two lakes, but mostly you'll find the fish to be using altogether different types of areas. Since the walleyes will move into their summer patterns first in Lake Weed Walleye, let's look at the spots where we would expect to find the most walleyes during the summer in this lake.

Walleye location in a body of water such as Lake Weed Walleye revolves primarily around one feature: WEEDS. The best weed for walleyes, and most species of fish, is the cabbage weed. Cabbage is found in many lakes throughout walleye country and is a major locational element in many lakes.

There are a couple of reasons why good weeds are so important to walleyes in water systems such as Lake Weed Walleye. One important reason is that they provide cover for the fish. Lake Weed Walleye doesn't have much structure for the walleyes to relate to, and not much depth that the fish can sink into when light penetration gets intense. The cabbage provides an umbrella that filters out the sun's rays, and also gives the fish something to relate to, much like a pile of rocks.

Another feature that draws the walleyes to the vegetation is the abundance of forage. Most of the baitfish that call Lake Weed Walleye home hold in or near the weeds. The walleyes don't have to go far to look for a meal. Wherever old marble eyes lives, you can bet that in the summer, if baitfish are around, walleyes won't be too far away.

Where to start on a body of water like Lake Weed Walleye? We'll be fishing weeds, but there are so many areas with vegetation that we need to narrow down the potential fish holding

areas.

For starters, we'll try to pinpoint the small rock and gravel humps that the walleyes used for spawning. There will still be fish using these areas. In fact, the hard bottom areas near weeds will hold walleyes year 'round. The humps that are closest to shore will be used more early in the year. As summer progresses, the humps and islands that are farther off shore will hold more fish than they did earlier, although the close-in humps will still be used. When you can find hard bottom areas that butt up next to the cabbage, you'll have walleyes near-by. Unfortunately, bodies of water such as Lake Weed Walleye don't have all that many rock humps or suitable hard bottom areas. We're going to have to work the weedlines to find action after we've tried the firmer bottom areas.

One of the keys to success in fishing a weedline is to work the irregularities. The points and pockets in the weeds are going to be locations where the fish concentrate. You can go out and spend an hour working a straight weedline and take a few fish, or you can pull up on a point in the weedline and pop five or six walleyes in just a few minutes. Same's true for a pocket in the weedline. The irregularities are where the fish will be. It works well to hit a point or pocket, take the fish you can, and move to another point or pocket. On a straight weedline, you'll usually find a straggler here and another one a little farther down, and if you spend enough time on that weedline a few fish will be caught. By fishing just the points and pockets, you're spending your time where most of the fish are, and you'll end up catching more fish in less time.

During the day, the walleyes will usually be on the shaded side of the point and near the bottom, especially in the summer. On overcast days or at dawn and dusk, they could be on either side of the point and higher off the bottom. They can even be found from time to time working over the tops of the weeds during low-light conditions. When they move to the tops of the cabbage, they can be very easy to catch.

If you're working a particular spot on a point and getting a lot of panfish pecks, try moving to the other side of the point or a little deeper or shallower. The walleyes are probably in the general area, but not right in there with the panfish. Move around, but don't wander too far away from the point and you'll eventually find where the predators are.

Walleyes can be found on the deep weedline or the shallow weedline, but most of the time most of them will be on the deep weedline. If you were to start on shore and wade out into the lake, the area where you first start to find cabbage would be the shallow weedline. If you were to continue the cabbage growth would get heavier and the water would get deeper. Eventually you would get to a point where the weed growth stopped as the water continued to get deeper. This area is what we refer to as the deep weedline. In lakes with clear water, the deep weedline will usually be found deeper; in stained water systems the deep weedline will be found shallower. Most people who make commercial lake-maps include a secchi-disc reading. A secchi-disc is a device used to determine water clarity. The disc is lowered into the lake on a string, and the depth at which it disappears is noted on the map. If the disc disappears at nine feet, the lake has a secchi-disc reading of nine feet. We've found that by doubling the secchi-disc reading, you can usually get a pretty good idea, within a couple of feet, of how deep the deep weedline will be. In a lake with a secchi-disc reading of five, the deep weedline will usually be around ten feet. A little work with a sonar unit will reveal the exact depth at which the weedline occurs.

As mentioned earlier, walleyes will most commonly be found on the deep weedline. However, there are situations when they

can be found and caught on the shallow weedline, also known as the inside weedline. One of these situations is when an oxygen depletion pushes the fish out of the deeper water. The walleyes will occasionally swim through the oxygen-rich weeds right into the inside weedline area. That's where a lot of the baitfish will be, therefore that's where the walleyes will be. At times it's possible to visually spot the loose groups of walleyes cruising the shallows of the inside weedline.

Fishing pressure will also cause the walleyes to move to the shallow weedline. If there are a bunch of boats on the deep weedline and the walleyes move, sometimes they'll go shallow. Although the fish will most often use the deep weedline, be aware that there are situations when walleyes can be found and caught near the shallow cabbage and sandgrass edges.

Walleyes will use clumps of weeds just like they use a weedline, but clumps can be much easier to fish. Coontail is a type of weed that grows in clumps, and although it usually isn't as good a fish-holding weed as cabbage, we have taken a bunch of walleyes from this specie of vegetation.

Clumps of coontail can be easily and quickly fished. Again, look for the irregularity in the weeds. Maybe there's a small point going off to one side of the clump. Maybe two individual clumps of coontail are connected by one narrow band of weeds. Try to find a spot where some cabbage is growing in or near the coontail. That can be a real hot-spot! If the clusters of coontail are small enough, it doesn't take long to fish your way around the weeds, but if a large stand of coontail is encountered, your time will be spent much more productively working the irregularities.

As summer progresses, the two shallow sunken islands will finally become productive. There could be a few walleyes on them early in the year, but they will be best from mid to late sum-

mer. The island on the west side of the lake tops out at eight fee-tand is rock-capped, the east side island has cabbage growing on and around it. The rock-capped island might be better on an overcast day, while the cabbage island will be more productive on a bright day. The cabbage will provide more shade for the fish under bright conditions, so they may be feeding more actively, especially on the shaded side of the cabbage, under bright conditions. The rocks don't provide much shade, so the walleyes will sit tight until light penetration decreases. Cloud cover, wind, or the sun dropping lower in the sky will be what it takes to turn those fish on.

In the summer, jigs, live-bait rigs, crankbaits and spinners will all take fish on Lake Weed Walleye, and we'll be either casting or trolling these lure types depending on current conditions. At times, one angler in the boat might be casting while the other trolls. Presentation is an important consideration once you've located the walleyes.

Let's start out talking about jigs. Jigs will catch walleyes spring, summer, and fall in Lake Weed Walleye, but it's import-

Copyright Pro-Mo's Secrets, Inc., Dec. 1989

The effects of fishing pressure. We're fishing a small hump all by ourselves and catching one walleye after another. More boats move in and all of the sudden the fish are bombarded with baits, anchors and a lot of overhead activity. When this happens, the fish move off the structure or drop to the bottom and become hard to catch.

ant to understand when these baits will be most productive, and which style will be best.

Sixteenth and eighth ounce jigs will be the sizes most commonly used. If we were limited to one jig weight, it would be, without question, the eighth ounce size for this type body of water.

Experiment with color and color patterns. We like jigs with some orange, yellow, or chartreuse in them, but we've taken so many walleyes on jigs of other colors. The best advice we can offer is to keep trying the different colors and combinations of colors until the best one is found. Sometimes the fish will show a color preference, sometimes they won't. Color preference can change from day to day and hour to hour, so if a productive color stops producing, try something else.

The jigs can be either cast or trolled, but we will probably cast them more on a lake of this type than any other. The shallow rock humps are fairly small areas and will be more effectively worked by casting. It's easier to cover the hump more thoroughly by anchoring or slowly working around the hump with an electric motor and casting the jig to the suspected fish-holding area. Trolling over the top of the hump won't give much coverage with the bait, and the boat going overhead could spook the walleyes.

When the walleyes are right on the edge of the weedline, casting or a controlled drift will be more effective. Trolling will work, but it's tough to keep the jig right on the edge of the weeds where the fish are. If the bait gets a little too deep, the fish don't hit. If the bait gets up in the weeds, snags can result. By casting, it's possible to put almost every cast right on the edge of the weeds where the fish are. Sure you'll still get some snags, but that's inevitable.

At times, the walleyes will suspend along the weedline. They might be seven feet from the water's surface and five feet off the bottom. If you're getting a lot of strikes as the jig is sinking, the fish are suspended. Using a slower falling jig will keep the bait in the fish zone longer and probably increase the number of strikes you get. Use a lighter jig, or put a larger than ordinary plastic body on the jig. The larger body will create more water resistance and make the jig fall slower.

Light jigs tipped with a plastic tail work well when the walleyes are cruising above the tops of the weeds. Swim this jig/tail combo so it ticks the tops of the vegetation, sometimes letting it sink a foot or so into the weeds. This technique can be dynamite when the fish are in this position.

Live-bait rigs are also walleye foolers when the fish are in a position that makes them susceptible to rigs. We'll usually back-troll the typical slip sinker live-bait rig when the walleyes are

holding deeper than the weedline. If the deep weedline is at ten feet, sometimes the fish will hold in twelve to fourteen feet. They're close to the weedine but not right on it. The rigs can be trolled because the walleyes are holding in an area where the cabbage won't create a snag problem. Trolling rigs work best if you can find a hump, point, or some sort of structure just off the weedline.

Todd Amenrud was pre-fishing a tournament when this lunker inhaled a Rainbow Spinner and crawler. Who says you can't take big walleyes in the summer? Todd released this fish and another one about the same size in hopes of catching them during the tournament. He didn't. That's tournament fishing, right Todd?

If two or three anglers are working this technique from the same boat, it oftentimes will add weight to your stringer to have one of the fishermen casting a jig or crankbait toward the weed-line. By doing so, you're covering more water and different potential fish-holding areas, and increasing the chances of putting your bait near a walleye that will bite.

When the walleyes are on the bottom at the edge of the weeds, and if jigs don't seem to be doing the job, try a live bait

rig with a twelve to eighteen inch snell. Tip this rig with a leech, minnow, or crawler, and cast it to the edge of the weedline. Let it sink to the bottom, then retrieve slowly, giving the bait plenty of five second rests. Sometimes this is what it takes to get a walleye to open it's mouth.

Crankbaits are also fish-catchers when the walleyes are near the weeds. Cast a minnow-imitating floater over the tops of the weeds at the appropriate time and get ready to have the rod ripped from your hands. Cast or troll a deep-running crankbait along the deep weedline and you'll also catch fish. Try to match the running depth of the bait to the depth at which the fish are holding. If the walleyes are near the bottom, select a lure that runs within a foot or two of the bottom. When the fish move up within five to seven feet of the surface, use a bait that only runs down that far. Put the cranker near the walleyes and much of the time they'll hit.

There you have our advice on where to find walleyes in the summer in lakes where weeds are a major locational factor for the fish. Remember that hard bottom areas near vegetation and irregularities in the weed growth are going to concentrate old marble eyes. Find areas such as this, put a bait down there, and get ready to catch fish. Now let's talk about finding walleyes in the summer in the perfect body of water for walleyes, Lake Lotsa Walleyes.

SUMMER WALLEYES IN LAKE LOTSA' WALLEYES

Lake Lotsa' Walleyes has a wider variety of structural elements than Lake Weed Walleye. In the summer, the walleyes in this ideal lake can be in a number of locations, and frequently they will be found in completely different types of structures.

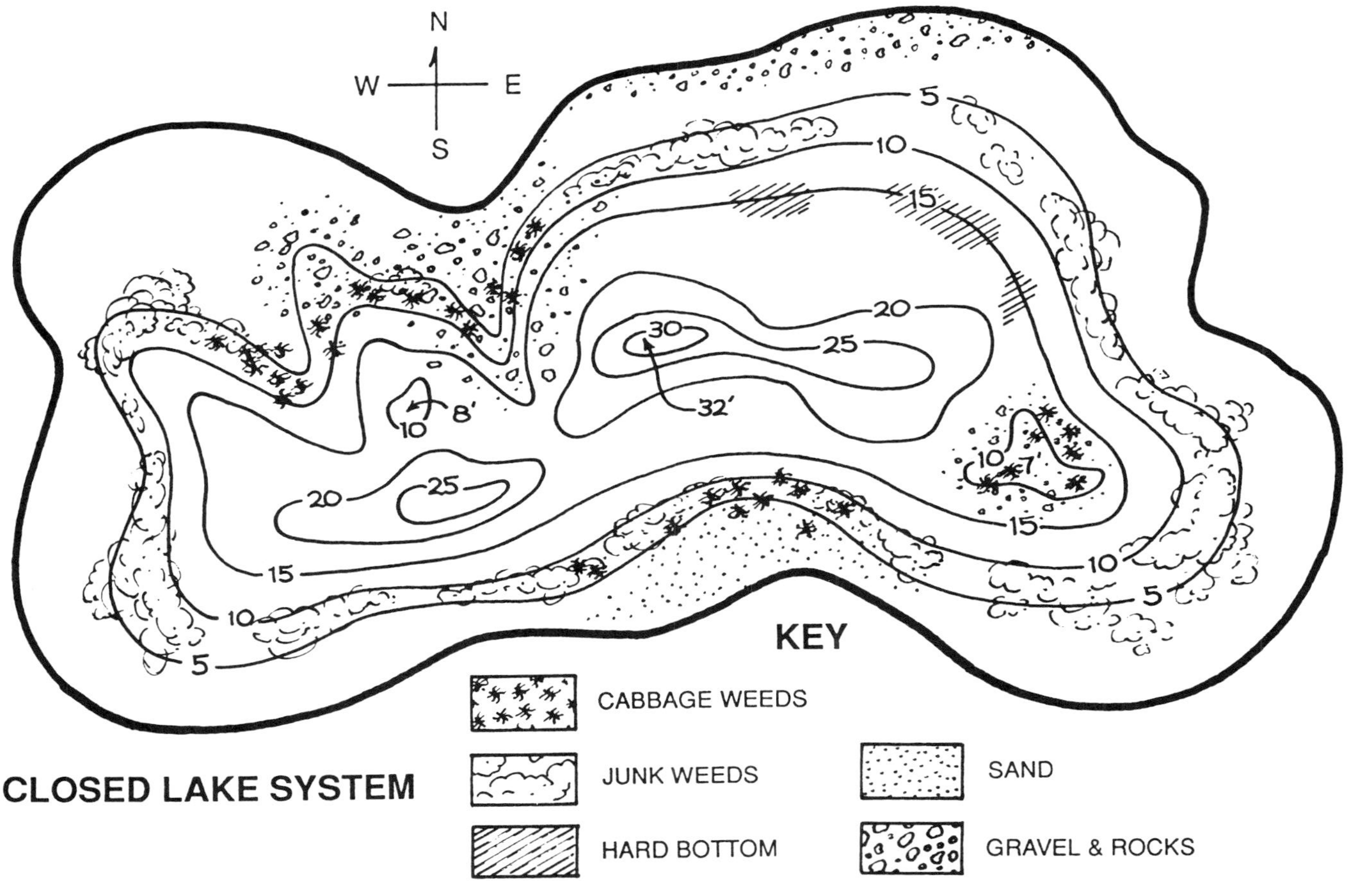

KEY

CABBAGE WEEDS

JUNK WEEDS

HARD BOTTOM

SAND

GRAVEL & ROCKS

CLOSED LAKE SYSTEM

N
W — E
S

Copyright Pro-Mo's Secrets, Inc., Dec. 1989

67

There will be some deep fish, some shallow fish, and some in-between fish. Some walleyes will be in the weeds, some will be on the breaks, and others will be over rock-capped humps. Our goal is to find the areas where the most fish will be most easily caught. It's important to keep that concept in mind. Find the areas where the most fish will be most easily caught. You may find a huge school of walleyes over a sunken island but they don't bite. At the same time there are scattered walleyes along a point. There aren't as many fish along the point, but they will hit. Go after the biters. Although the point doesn't hold as many fish, you will probably catch more just because those fish are more aggressive. Remember to go back to that big school of walleyes on the hump though and check them every now and then. Eventually they will become active. With that in mind, let's talk about where old marble eyes will spend the summer in Lake Lotsa' Walleyes.

Early in the summer, look for walleyes near their spawning grounds. They usually don't abandon those areas immediately after the spawn. In fact, some of the areas used for spawning will hold fish year'round. Most of the points that the walleyes used for spawning will be all year residences for at least some fish, especially if there is access to deep water near by. Points B, C, and F are all good holding areas for gold-sided fish. The only difference between spring and summer is the walleyes location on these points. In the spring the fish were in the shallows on top of these structures. In the summer, they will be holding most of the time along the drop-offs on these points. On an overcast day or at night they might move up, but most of the time they will be found deeper than they were in the spring. Take into consideration the wind velocity and direction, light penetration, where the shade is, and you'll probably be where most of the catchable walleyes are.

The twelve foot sunken island directly off the mouth of the creek on the north shore will hold some fish early in the summer, and will probably be home to a few fish all the time, but frequently this will be just a stopping off spot. The walleyes that spawned in the vicinity of the creek will pull back to this spot after egg-laying and hang around for awhile, then continue to other areas such as Point B or F, or to the weedline in Area G. Give the spot a hit, but don't spend too much time here UNLESS the creek becomes swollen due to heavy rains. If the creek starts pumping a lot of water into the lake and the current increases quite a bit, fish will be drawn back into this area. A bunch of fish will go right up into the creek, but others will relate to the sunken island, especially after the stream starts to go back to its normal level and current flow.

It's been our experience that in a body of water such as this, the different sizes of walleyes will relate to the different areas. Weed and weedline walleyes will be on the smallish side, maybe up to two and a half pounds, with an occasional bigger fish thrown in. The walleyes that inhabit the area from the deep weedline down the breaks will be larger, frequently up to four pounds, with more big fish being found in this area than in the shallows. Trophy size walleyes will be most abundant along the deep breaks and near sunken islands. We've also found that there are lots of big walleyes suspended over open water. They might suspend near the points or sunken islands and move to the structure when it comes time to feed, or they might suspend near ciscoes, perch, shad, or tullibees and grab one of them when the urge strikes. Yes, there are times when a school of lunker walleyes will move en masse onto a shallow point, and there are also periods when the smaller fish will move deeper. Interestingly, the smaller walleyes frequently move deeper when the big walleyes move shallow. Most of the time though, in this type of lake, the walleyes will be found in the summer in the areas just described. With that in mind let's take a look at a few key locations on the map and determine how they would most effectively be fished.

Areas B, C, E, and F would be fished very similarly. Point B doesn't have weeds so the drop-offs would be worked. Go over the area keeping a close eye on your sonar. When a depth or depth range is spotted where there seems to be an abundance of fish life, note that depth and give it a shot. Irregularities on the structure will also concentrate the fish. If there is a finger extending from the point, or an area where the drop-off is sharper than anywhere else on the point, that could be a good spot to try.

Areas C and F are similar. They both have a weedline and deep water nearby. The walleyes could be near the weedline, on the breaks, or in Area C, on the sunken island just off the tip of the point. Fish the different areas and watch the sonar to find out where most of the walleye activity is. The sunken island could be the best big fish spot on this body of water. It's near a spawning area and deep water. Forage in the form of cisco and tullibee will be nearby in the deep water. This is our choice for the best big fish spot on the lake.

A few words about sunken islands. They can be dynamite spots, but sometimes they're productivity is over-emphasized. For the sunken island to be a consistent producer, it should have a few features. First, it shouldn't be too small. Small islands will hold a few fish, but usually there won't be enough space for very many walleyes. Small sunken islands close to other structures will usually be more productive than a small island out all by itself. The remote hump might hold a few fish, but the hump close to other structures will hold more fish consistently.

A good sunken island will have several other characteristics. An island with some cabbage, some rocks, fingers extending from

it, and breaks with different degrees of drop-off will enhance the fish attracting qualities of the structure. A sunken island that tops off at one level then drops right back down again will not be as productive as a multi-structured island.

When working areas B, C, E, and F, remember to consider the variables we talked about earlier. If the wind is blowing from the south, we would probably look at Point B as the best starting spot. The south side of Point F could also be good. If it's mid-morning, there isn't much wind and the sun is bright, the west side of Point C would be a good starting location because of the shade factor.

Location D will hold fish, but they'll probably be scattered. Some of the walleyes will be up in the weeds, others will be along the breaks. It's an area that will produce fish, especially on an overcast day. Area D isn't a primary walleye-attracting spot, but if the better structures on the lake are getting fished heavily, it could produce.

Area G is essentially a weedline and there will be fish here. It isn't an area that will hold lots of big fish, but it's a good bet for some action. This area would be worked the same way we fished Lake Weed Walleye. Look for the points and pockets in the weeds, as well as the areas where different types of weeds join the cabbage. Try backtrolling the drop-off right along the deep edge of the cabbage. On a cloudy day the walleyes might move over the tops of the weeds. Basically, look for the fish in Area G to be in the same weed locations as they were on Lake Weed Walleye.

A phenomena that occurs on many lakes in early to mid summer is a mayfly hatch. This occurrence can create tough fishing conditions for a few days because more food is added to the food-chain. If possible, we would suggest that you try a different body of water where the walleye's eating opportunities are more limited.

If moving to another lake isn't an option, don't give up hope. By understanding how the mayfly hatch works, it's still possible to take some fish.

Adult mayflies lay their eggs on the surface of the water. The eggs sink, gathering on plants, rocks, and other elements found on the bottom of the lake. Some time after hatching, the mayflies begin rising toward the surface of the lake. Evidently mayflies are a delicacy to the walleyes, because they follow them closely as they rise. Walleyes are normally thought of as a fish that feeds on or near the bottom. During a mayfly hatch, however, they frequently suspend and wait for the insects as they rise to the surface. In fact, it's not uncommon to see a walleye suck a mayfly off the surface of the water. Catching walleyes during a hatch can be tough, but not impossible if you get your bait closer to the surface.

We often hear how difficult walleye catching can be during the dog-days of summer. We've found that most of the time in the summer, poor action can be attributed to not finding the fish. A walleye's metabolism is higher in the summer, therefore the fish must eat more. Much of the time if you can put a bait near a glassy-eyed fish, they'll hit.

The key to catching walleyes is to fish where they are. How many times have you been on a lake in the spring and just hammered the fish on one particular spot? Go back a month or two later and the area is void of fish. They've moved, and if you want to catch walleyes, you'll have to move too.

Another happening that can make fishing tougher in the summer is the increased number of baitfish. All the minnows and baitfish that were spawned in the spring are now at a size that the walleyes can feed on. More bait in the water means your lure presentation will have to be better. Keep moving until the fish are found, and be aware of lure presentation and you'll continue to

catch walleyes during the hottest part of the summer.

During the summer, look for the biggest walleyes to be near the areas of sunken islands and points with the sharpest drop-offs. This is frequently where the lunkers will be. In a lake with cisco and tullibees, the walleyes will trap these baitfish against the sharp-breaking areas. Walleyes "herd" the cisco and tullibees against the walls of these fast tapering breaks and the baitfish are unable to escape for a couple of reasons. First, they are sensitive to water temperatures. The warmer water near the top of the sunken island or point acts as a barrier, and typically the cisco or tullibee won't go into that warmer layer of water. The only other way out is to head back toward the open water and into the waiting jaws of the hungry walleyes. Usually the walleyes will suspend out from the break and move into the school of baitfish to feed, occasionally picking off a cisco or tullibee that wanders too far out. There will also usually be a few walleyes laying on or near the bottom along the break.

Just as the larger fish will inhabit the sharper breaks, the smaller ones will be most abundant near the more gradual tapers. The tullibee and cisco are too big for two pound walleyes to feed on, and a two pound walleye is just the right size for a larger walleye to feed on. Look for the smaller fish to be on the slower breaking drop-offs.

Now that we've got a good idea of where the walleyes are going to be during the summer, how do we catch them. In Lake Weed Walleye, jigs were used a lot. Jigs will produce on Lake Lotsa' Walleye, but the fish will also like other presentations just as well. Walleyes on Lake Lotsa' Walleyes will start hitting live-bait rigs sooner than on the weed lake. Rigs allow for a more natural presentation, and with the abundance of forage and clearer water, the more natural presentation will be more productive. Jigs will still produce in the weeds, but when working the breaks and

deep water, the rigs might be a better first choice.

Deep Transition Lines

In late summer and early fall the walleyes will trap baitfish against steep drop-offs. Pulling Shad-Raps through these areas is a great way to take lots of fish. We've caught loads of 5-8 pound Walleyes on #9 Shad Raps when the walleyes were in this position.

Here we also have a deep transition line. Again, bottom content has changed. In the deeper areas, the transition is frequently from sand to muck, although in some lakes it will be from small rocks to sand.

When using live-bait rigs, pay attention to the sonar. If the fish are showing up on the unit several feet off the bottom, increase the snell length so the bait gets up to the fish. If the fish are up quite a ways, try an air-injected nightcrawler on the rig. Air-injected crawlers ride higher than leeches or minnows, making it easier to get the bait up to the fish.

On the other hand, sometimes the fish will be tight to the bottom. If this is the case, shorten the snell length and drop the bait

right into the fishes face. When you don't know how long the snell should be, guess on the long side. It's better to have the bait a little over the walleyes than under them, as fish are more likely to move up for a bait than move down.

If you're sure the fish are on a particular point or break, but not sure exactly where, a bottom-bouncer/spinner rig is an effective tool for covering water. Quickly work the suspected fish-holding area with the spinner to find the fish. After they've been found, it frequently pays to slow down and strain the location with a rig.

Suspended fish can be caught using a couple of different techniques. Usually when the fish are suspended they'll spread out. The trick is to cover a lot of water and put a bait near as many fish as possible. You can usually get a few to open their mouths. We like to use crankbaits in this situation whether the fish are relating to a mayfly hatch or are holding near a school of tullibee or cisco. The crankbaits allow us to cover water quickly, and big walleyes have a strong willingness to hit cranks.

Select the size of crankbait to use by determining how deep the fish are. If a lot of fish are seen on sonar ten feet below the surface, use a bait that runs to about that depth. If they're deeper use a deeper running bait, if they're shallower, use a shallower running lure. In some lakes in the summer it's common to find the walleyes fifteen to twenty-five feet below the surface, with the depth being 150 feet. We've caught a lot of these fish using the biggest, deepest diving crankbaits available. Don't worry about using a too large bait in the summer. Frequently trophy walleyes prefer the bigger ones.

Color can be important, but don't let it be an over-riding concern. We've taken a ton of suspended walleyes on natural shad, silver/black back, and chartreuse plugs. Experiment until a productive color is discovered.

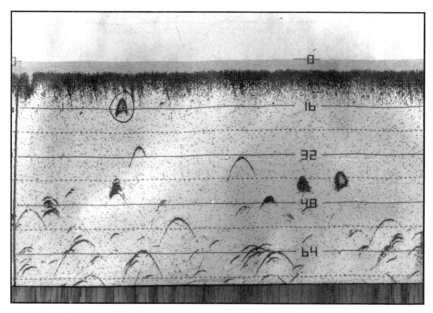

Do walleyes suspend? You bet they do! This graph paper proves it. The water is over a hundred feet deep, yet many of the walleyes are within 50 feet of the surface. The circled fish at the 16 foot line is a biter and can be caught. The deeper fish will be more susceptible to a bait when they move closer to the surface. The Lowrance X-16 paper graph we use draws a beautiful picture of the watery underworld and has helped us put fish in the boat in many situations.

If the fish are suspended and confined to a particular area, a slip bobber can be good. The slip bobber allows a bait to be presented at a precise depth and worked slowly, and if you know exactly where the walleyes are, can be deadly. However, bobbers really shine when the walleyes move shallow over wind-blown points and reefs.

We've got the walleyes located and we know how to catch them. It's important that we are able to stay on the active fish. When a fish is caught, it's imperative that we cover that areathoroughly, but many anglers don't. They net the fish and just keep

76

moving, leaving a school of hungry walleyes behind. Staying on the fish can be the difference between continuous action and scattered action.

As soon as a fish hits, glance at the depth-finder to note the depth. Then try to pick out an object on the shoreline to use as a mark. We prefer to line up two objects on shore, maybe a flag-pole right in line with the front door of the red house. Now you can return to the spot where the fish hit.

If there are no distinguishing landmarks and you've popped three or four fish, you might want to throw a marker. We don't put a marker out unless the spot holding the fish is small and we're having trouble getting back onto the exact area. If it's tough finding the hot-spot, don't waste time trying to relocate it after each fish, throw a marker.

Randy Amenrud with one of those suspended walleyes. Notice the long rod Randy's using? To get a #9 Shad Rap down to the fish, it was necessary to use 6 lb. test XL. The shock absorbing qualities of the 8'6" Series One Steelhead rod prevented the line from breaking on the strike, and was also more comfortable to hang on to. This fish was taken 18 feet down over 140 feet of water.

Don't place the marker right on the hot-spot, throw it shallower and mentally note the location of the marker in relation to the fish-holding area. We throw the marker shallower for two rea-

Use marker buoys as a reference point. Don't throw them on the school of fish, throw the marker shallower than where the fish are located. Markers can attract fishermen, but at times they're necessary to keep track of the fish.

sons. First, there's less chance of a hooked fish getting tangled up in the marker because hooked fish usually swim toward deeper water. Secondly, there are some folks who think that the marker was thrown to mark the fish for them. We don't mind sharing an area with other people, but when fishin's tough, too many boats going right over the fish can spook them.

Also pay attention to the way the fish takes the bait. If it hits and continues moving slowly along, it's probably swimming with the school. Note the direction in which the fish is moving because that's probably the way the school is moving. If you want to stay on the fish, you should move in the same direction

as the school.

If the fish smacks the bait and runs quickly, it could mean there is a school of active walleyes holding on that spot. The fish hit and ran quickly to get away from the school. Fish will try to take the bait away from each other. After the fish is landed, cast right back to the spot where it hit.

When a fish hits and doesn't move very much, it could mean a stationary school has been located. It also means that the fish aren't real aggressive. A slow moving lure will probably be best.

Summer is a great time to catch lots of walleyes. They are generally quite active, and when you find them action can be fast. More people fish for walleyes in the summer than any other season, and by keeping in mind the things we've just talked about about, you should be able to have some hot action during the warmest season.

Chapter 8

Walleyes in Lakes

Autumn-Trophy Time

The autumn season is a wonderful time to be outside, and if you're going to be outside, you might as well be chasing walleyes. Many outdoors-people trade their rods for rifles and shotguns in the fall, and we don't blame them. However, if you don't spend some time on the water in pursuit of glassy-eyed fish, you're missing some of the best action of the year. The lakes are uncrowded, so you can have the best spots all to yourself. Best of all, the fish are frequently active and easy to catch. Also, your chances of taking a walleye of wall-hanging proportions are better now than almost any other time of year. What more incentive does an person need to go fishing?

Versatility is the key to success in the fall. The walleyes will be found in the shallows, at mid-range depths, and down deep.

Bright, warm days are preferred to cold, blustery ones. The sun is lower in the sky this time of year, so light penetration is decreased. However, bright days will cause the water to warm up, which will turn the fish on. Frequently, action will be better from mid-day on.

In early fall, many lakes undergo a change that can create difficult fishing for a few days. This change is called the turnover, and it seems to disorient the walleyes. The turnover is caused by a change in water temperature. During the summer, water temps are warmer on the surface of the lake. As fall approaches, air temperatures go down which eventually cause the water temperature on the surface of the lake to go down. When the surface temperature of the water reaches the point where it's cooler than

Duane Held and his fishing partner swing aboard their morning's catch. Duane owns Paradise Cove, a resort in Minaki, Ontario, that is located on some of the best drive-in walleye fishing we've ever seen.

the water below it, the upper layer and lower layer of water flip-flop positions. The surface water that has now cooled sinks, the now warmer lower layer of water rises. Thus the phenomena of turnover.

After the turnover, water temperatures stabilize, giving the walleyes a lot of freedom of movement. As mentioned earlier, sometimes they'll be shallow, sometimes they'll be deep, and other times they'll be somewhere between the two. The trick is to find where most of the active fish are. Let's take a look at our two walleye lakes and see where we can expect to find most of the action in the fall.

FALL WALLEYES IN
LAKE WEED WALLEYE

In the spring, the walleyes in this smaller, shallower body of water became active before the fish in Lake Lotsa' Walleyes. In the fall, the walleyes in Lake Weed Walleye will shut off earlier also. Just as this lake warmed up earlier in the spring, it will cool off sooner in the fall. Early autumn can provide some good fishing in this lake, however.

The best areas in the fall will be the same as in the spring and summer. The fish will be relating to the hard bottom areas, the points, and the turns and irregularities in the weedline. There just aren't enough options in structure in this lake to move the fish around very much. An important consideration is this. The green weeds will be far more productive in any lake in the fall than the dying brown ones. The green weeds are still giving off oxygen, which attracts the baitfish, which in turn attract hungry walleyes. The walleyes that are weed-oriented will be drawn to the remaining green cabbage in a big way.

If there is a swamp or marshy area near this body of water,

there could be a frog migration from the swamp to the lake. When this migration occurs, expect the walleyes to be in the shallows waiting for the frogs. The fish will move into just a couple feet of water at this time, and they can be very easy to catch. Some rainy, early fall evening take a drive down a road between the lake and the marsh. If there are a lot of frogs on the road, get a rod out, tie on a crankbait, jig, or rig and a frog and go fishing. Night fishing will usually be more productive, especially if the water in the lake is fairly clear.

In Lake Weed Walleyes jigs, rigs, and crankbaits will all produce in the fall. It will frequently be best to tip the jigs and rigs with minnows, but leeches will also produce, especially in the afternoon after the water has had a chance to warm up. When the fish are pin-pointed, such as they will be on the weed points and pockets, it works better to cast jigs. Casting makes it possible to throw directly to the fish-holding area, thereby keeping the bait close to the walleyes as much as possible.

Finding the walleyes in the fall, or any other time of year for that matter, on shallow, weedy bodies of water such as Lake Weed Walleyes is no real secret. Work the same general areas you've been working all year and eventually the fish will be found. Remember that the fish in many lakes of this type will become more difficult to catch as the fall progresses. When they get too tough, consider spending more time on a deeper, clearer, more multi-structured lake such as Lake Lotsa' Walleyes.

FINDING FALL WALLEYES IN LAKE LOTSA' WALLEYES

Moving around and covering water is the key to finding and catching walleyes in the fall in a lake such as this. In the spring the fish were most abundant in the shallows, in the summer they spread out a little more, but in the autumn old marble eyes will

go just about wherever they want to. During this time of year, the baitfish and panfish start pulling away from the shallows and weeds because those areas are getting too cold. The walleyes are going to be near the forage, and that's where we should be too.

In the fall, we'll probably see some minnows using the incoming creek on the north shore. If the minnows are in the creek, you can bet the walleyes will be there as well. Usually this area will produce better at night when the fish swim right into the mouth of the creek. During the day the walleyes will hold along the breaks just off the mouth of the creek. If your lake has an incoming creek, check it during the day for the presence of baitfish. If you see schools of shiners or other types of minnows, come back at night and you'll probably be able to catch walleyes. Be prepared to put in some time the first few nights until you get the pattern down. In many situations such as this, the fish will move in, feed heavily for maybe half an hour, then pull out of the area. A little later another school will move through. It's possible to put together a pattern and predict with some accuracy when the walleyes will move in.

There's a lot of options open to the walleyes on Lake Lotsa' Walleyes. At the same time there will be fish shallow on the points, along the breaks of the points, on the weedline, and around the sunken island off Point C. Don't get hung up fishing just one area or one type of structure.

Start off the day looking for old marble eyes along the breaks off the points. Run the breaks with the boat, keeping a close eye on the depth-finder. Note the depth where most of the fish activity seems to be. Start off at that depth, but don't hesitate to go deeper or shallower.

As the day progresses, the fish can move. On a bright, warm day, don't be surprised if the walleyes move shallow. Remember,

When the walleyes move into the shallows at night in the fall, it doesn't take many lures to catch them. A small tackle box that fits in the pocket of a jacket or your waders with a few Rapalas, Shad Raps, and some three inch Power Grubs and eighth ounce jig heads are all it takes to fool a lunker.

light penetration in the fall isn't as great as in the summer. The sun isn't directly overhead in the fall, so the light penetration is at more of an angle. As the water warms, the fish can move into water just two to six feet deep, and they frequently will do so in the fall. Look for this to happen most commonly on sun-drenched shorelines. Points that are warming can be exceptionally good. On days when not much warming is taking place, look for the fish to stay out on the breaks in deeper water. They will move parallel

Bob Jensen with a ten pound walleye and a bonus bass taken off a deep weedline in the fall. Most species of fish go on a feeding binge in the fall, and if you're there at the right time, you'll take big fish.

to shore, but usually not much shallower or deeper. Keep in mind the tips we suggested for staying on the fish and you'll be able to catch these breakline walleyes all day long.

The sunken island off of Point C will still be a hog hot-spot. These fish probably won't move around as much as those fish closer to shore. They may move from one side of the island to the other, and they might go from for example, the forty foot level to the top of the island, but frequently they won't be affected as much by minor changes in weather as the shallower fish will.

The walleyes in Area G can be caught, especially if you find a sharp break that sweeps in close to the weedline. A sharp break will tend to concentrate the fish, while a gradual taper could cause them to spread out a little more.

Night fishing can be very productive, especially if you're looking for a big fish, and the fall is arguably the best time to look for a trophy at night. Areas A and B will be the favored locations for trolling crankbaits. Point B is chosen over the other points because it is void of weed growth and has access to deep water. In late fall, ciscoes and tullibees move into areas such as this to spawn, and walleyes will follow them. When the ciscoes and tullibees move onto the top of the point at night, a feeding frenzy can occur. These fall -spawning baitfish will also drop their eggs on the other points in the weed growth, but trolling crankbaits in the weeds can be a difficult task due to snagging.

Trolling or casting jigs and rigs will be our preferred methods of presentation. Jigs probably will account for more fish, but rigs will be a very close second. Crankbaits can also be excellent fish-takers, and frequently they will account for some of the largest walleyes. Gear your lure to the situation encountered and you are going to catch walleyes.

There you have many of our secrets for finding walleyes in lakes in the spring, summer and fall. If it seems like we covered walleye

location in the summer more heavily, we did. More people chase walleyes in the summer than any other time, and most anglers indicate that they have more trouble catching gold-sided fish in the summer than any other time of the year. That's why we devoted more of the lake portion of this book to summer fishing. Besides, much of the walleye location in the summer is applicable to walleye location in the fall.

You may also say that the walleye lakes we've talked about aren't like the lakes you fish. We're aware of that too. In fact, if you know of a lake that's the same as Lake Lotsa' Walleyes, let us know, we would like to fish there. However, we're sure that whatever lake you fish, it probably has several of the structural elements we've included in our lakes, and if you work these structures at the times we've suggested, and using the techniques mentioned, you will take walleyes. With all that in mind, let's talk about finding and catching walleyes in rivers.

Chapter 9

Sometimes The Best Bet
For Action

There are lots of good reasons to fish for walleyes in rivers. Rivers are everywhere, and most of them have anywhere from fair to excellent populations of walleyes and, in some cases, sauger. As a matter of fact, walleyes are by nature a resident of flowing water. In lakes that are fed by rivers or streams, as we've discussed, walleyes are drawn to the incoming current at various times of the year. Besides, most anglers live close to a river, and therefore it's easy for us to get onto some good walleye water when the urge strikes.

Fish in rivers seem to be less affected by adverse weather conditions than their lake-dwelling cousins. After a cold front has blown through and walleyes in the local lakes are tough to catch, it's very possible to pull onto a hole in the river and pop a bunch

A typical river stretch with many of the structures talked about in the River Section.

1 - Wingdams-Man-made structures to direct the current away from the bank to prevent erosion. Also excellent walleye areas at different times of the year. In this river they can be found extending from the west bank and some islands.

2 - Rip-Rap - Another man-made structure to prevent shoreline erosion. Lots of it along the west bank and some islands.

3 - Side channel - Connects the main river with quieter back waters. Can be a fishy spot during certain river conditions.

4 - Mid-river structures - Water levels will determine when and how walleyes and sauger will use these areas.

The text in this section contains detailed information on when, where, and how walleyes and sauger use the various structures.

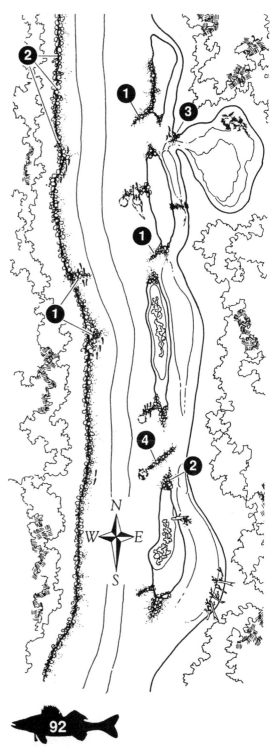

of fish. Perhaps it's the moving water that helps over-ride the effects of the weather. We aren't sure, but we do know that when action is slow on the lakes, a river is the place to be.

River fish are aggressive! This little guy took on a Shad Rap that was half his size, and this isn't uncommon on rivers. When a river walleye wants your bait, it's tough to keep it away from him.

Frequently, fish eat more in rivers than in lakes. When at rest the walleyes will usually move behind an object that breaks the flow of the current. When moving though, they are generally contending with the current. It requires more energy for the fish to swim upstream in a river than it does for a fish to move from spot to spot in a lake. The river fish burns more energy, so they have to eat more. The more they eat, the easier it is for us to catch them.

Those are several good reason for fishing for glassy-eyed fish in rivers. Fishing in rivers for walleyes, however, is different than fishing for walleyes in lakes. In lakes, structure is

a major locational factor. It is in rivers as well, but current also has a tremendous effect on the walleyes position, and food still has a lot to do with where the fish will be found.

Another concept to keep in mind is that river walleyes move around a lot. They can be in one location today, and another area tomorrow. They are extremely mobile at some times of the year, and if you want to have consistent action, flexibility and versatility are important. If the fish aren't where you caught them on the last trip, look somewhere else. At any one particular time we can expect to find a few walleyes in holes, some working wing-dams, a few running rip-rap, and more doing something else. What we're trying to do is find out what most of the active fish are doing. With that thought in mind, let's take a brief look at how walleyes move in rivers on an annual basis, then take a detailed look at how they relate to specific structural elements and current under different conditions.

A Walleye's Annual Movement in a River

In many areas throughout walleye country, the spring spawning run of walleyes is looked upon with the same anticipation as a child looking forward to Christmas. Anglers flock in droves to get choice spots on large and small rivers alike. Action can be very fast or very slow.

Most anglers are quite familiar with the spring spawning run. It's difficult to determine when the spring spawning run actually begins. While it's true that some walleyes in most all rivers will move upstream in the spring, in many rivers they move upstream in the fall and hold very near their spawning areas all winter. In the smaller rivers that have dams, the walleyes move to the dam area in mid-autumn and hold there until it's time to spawn in the spring. Other fish will hold in holes a little downstream, maybe a couple of miles below the dam, all winter, then move closer to

the dam in the spring.

In rivers that have a lock/dam system, the walleyes will move into the lock/dam area in the fall and hold there all winter. When the water starts warming in the spring, some of those fish will swim through the locks and continue upstream to the next lock system, while the other fish will spawn in the same general area where they spent the winter. These river walleyes can be real movers.

In the late-winter/early-spring, before the walleyes begin the spawning ritual, look for them in mid-river holes, on sand bars, and near bends in the channel. They'll probably be near the bottom and nosed in behind something that breaks the current. When they're in the holes they could be on the upstream or downstream side of the hole. Some sonar work might reveal where the majority of the walleyes are, but in rivers the walleyes and sauger usually hold tight to the bottom and frequently only the best paper graphs and LCGs will separate the fish from the bottom. At times it pays to work an area even if the sonar doesn't reveal the presence of fish.

When the water starts to warm, the fish will start to become more active and move shallower. The walleyes that held downstream all winter will start moving upstream and will use wingdams more. The wingdams serve mostly as stopping-off points for the walleyes however. The fish are moving toward the spawning grounds, and the wingdams are simply a rest stop. Fish can be caught here if you happen to hit a wingdam that's holding fish, but don't expect to find large numbers of walleyes holding on any particular wingdam for very long this time of year.

The fish will drop their eggs in a number of areas when the proper time arrives. Some will spread their eggs along sand and rubble shorelines, on rip-rap, and even in calm areas off the main current. The smaller males will still strike a bait now, but when the females go into the spawn, it will usually work out better if we search for areas that are holding fish that are still waiting to spawn or have already completed this annual occurrence.

When the walleyes are done spawning, most will immediately leave the spawning area. Some will travel a long distance upstream or downstream, others will move a short distance. Many marble-eyed fish will seek out slower current areas where they will spend several days just recovering from the rigors of the egg-dropping process.

Expect to find the fish using wing dams more after the spawn. Upon completing the spawn, many fish will drop down and hold for a few days on the wingdam closest to the spawning area. As time passes after the spawn, more fish will filter onto the wingdams farther downstream from the spawning area. Some fish will use the wingdams throughout the summer and into the fall, while others will find different areas to use.

Some of the other freshly spawned walleyes will slide into the cuts off the main channel. Again, most of these gold-sided fish are just looking for a place to rest and recover from spawning. They'll hold here a brief time, then move back toward the main channel and their summer areas, although there will be some walleyes that will work the back channels if there is current flow throughout the summer.

Old Marble Eyes will use a bunch of different types of areas in the summer. Some will use rip-rap, others will work wingdams, while shallower holes will also see some fish use. In general, summer fishing for walleyes can be a game of hide and seek. Most areas with rock, sand, and rubble will hold fish, the task is to find the locations that are holding the most active fish. The walleyes in the holes could be inactive, while the rip-rap fish are smacking. Obviously we would spend more time working the

rip-rap.

When the walleyes sense that the water temperature is starting to fall, they start to move back upstream. Now the wingdams far below the dam and near the summering grounds will hold the most fish. Walleyes begin using these wingdams first in the fall in their migration upstream. As the water cools, they move toward the dam, holding on wingdams as they go. The farther into fall the season progresses, the more the wingdams close to the dam see more fish use.

It isn't just the cooler water that causes the walleyes to move upstream. In rivers where shad are the primary source of food for the walleyes, a shad die-off occurs in the fall. The walleyes gather in huge schools immediately below the dam and gorge themselves on the shad that are coming through the dam. The best spots will be shallow rock piles and the eddies below the dam. The structures closest to the dam will often be best, but caution is advised. Most dams on major rivers have restricted areas anywhere from 150-300 feet below the dam. Many anglers will get as close to the dams as the law will permit, and they will, at times, fill the boat with fish.

When the water cools off even more, and the shad die-off is completed, the water usually clears up quite a bit. At this time, the walleyes will drop back into the deep holes and main channel areas and hold throughout the winter. The migration has come full circle, and the walleyes are ready to begin the entire process again in a few short months.

That's a simplified version of the movements of a walleye in a typical river. Although there will be minor variances in some moving water systems, most of the time the fish will react just as we've described. There are some factors that will influence which structures will be used at a given time, and where the walleyes will be on those structures. Let's take a look at specific things we'll look for in those locations.

Wingdams

Wingdams will hold walleyes all year long, although they won't be as good in the winter as in the other seasons. Here are some of our rules-of-thumb regarding wingdams.

The wingdams that consist of sand, rock, and a green, slimy substance are generally better than the ones that are just rock. The wingdams that have some sand are usually the older ones, and it seems that the longer the dam has been there, the better it is. However, beware of wingdams that are silted over. They're usually not very productive.

Wingdams that are on the outside edge of the river will be better, especially in the summer and fall. In rivers, the current will be washing into one bank harder than the other. The bank that the current is washing into is referred to as the outside edge. The wingdams on this edge are generally better because the current prevents the structure from being silted over, and more food is also swept into this area. Sometimes in the spring the wingdams on the inside edge will be more productive because the current is less, but most of the time the structures on the outside edge will be best.

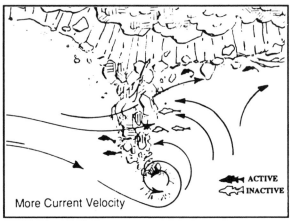

More Current Velocity

ACTIVE
INACTIVE

A top view of a wingdam in high water. The increased water velocity will cause most of the fish to be on the downstream side of the dam. The most active fish will be near the tip of the dam, and there will also be walleyes near the shore downstream from the dam.

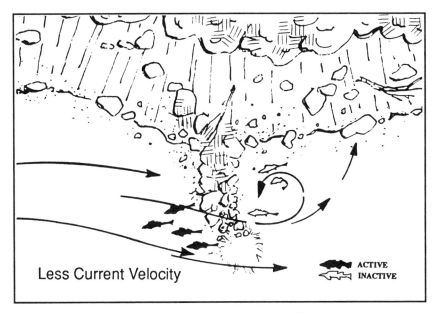

Less Current Velocity

ACTIVE
INACTIVE

The same wingdam during low water conditions. The current is decreased, so the walleyes will move around the dam more freely. The most active fish will still be on the upstream side of the structure however.

Water levels will play a large role in determining where the walleyes will be located on the wingdams. When the water is high and the current is fast, expect the fish to be on the downstream side of the dams and closer to shore. When water levels are low, the fish will frequently move to the tips of the dams, nearer to mid-river. If the water is high the fish will be tighter to the wingdam, when the water is low they might wander a little farther away. Remember, river fish position themselves according to the current. They hold in the lighter current areas just off the main flow. Fish in rivers don't fight the current, they use it. It doesn't take a very big object to break the flow of the water. A walleye will nose in behind a current-break such as a rock and just hold there. When a minnow or some other form of food comes around the rock, the fish will dart out, grab the bait, and move back behind the rock. Look for the walleyes in the slower water at the edge of the current.

A side view of a rock pile during low water. Less current velocity allows the fish to be near the top and upstream side of the structure. All these fish are in a position that would indicate they are catchable. Remember, the surface boil that reveals the presence of this structure will be slightly downstream from the structure during low water.

A side view of the same structure during high water. The most active fish will be the one on the upstream side of the rocks, and the one on top of the structure. The other three are probably going to be tougher to catch, although with exact lure presentation they could be taken. Hovering directly overhead and keeping a jig right in front of their face might be the best way to take the fish on the downstream side of the structure. In high water, the surface boil is going to be farther downstream from the structure than it would be in low water conditions.

When walleyes become active on wingdams, look for them to be on the top or upstream side of the structure. If shad and bait-fish are breaking the surface over one particular dam, that's probably where the fish are feeding and will be most easily caught. It could be white bass that are forcing the baitfish to the surface, but it could also be a hungry school of walleyes on the

prowl.

Schools of walleyes will also roam between wingdams. Instead of just running your boat from one dam to another, try trolling a crankbait at different depths between wingdams. If they're not on the dams, they're probably between them.

Many anglers locate the wingdams by watching along the bank for a line of riffles that extends from shore into the river. That's a good way to get a general location of the dam, but remember that the structure will actually be upstream of the riffles or boils. The deeper the water over the wing-dam, the farther downstream the riffles and boils will appear. Use a sonar to determine the exact position of the dam.

Many smaller and mid-size rivers don't have wingdams, yet they have natural structures that the walleyes will relate to just as they do to wingdams. Small rock points and humps will create slack water and riffles, and can be treated almost the same as a wingdam.

Rip-Rap

Rip-rap is large boulders placed along river banks to prevent the bank from eroding. Rip-rap has another benefit though. It attracts and holds walleyes in varying numbers most of the time. In the spring, old marble eyes will spread out on rip-rap banks to drop their eggs. At this time, they'll seek out rip-rap that is in an area of less current flow.

As the season progresses, the fish will most usually be concentrated on rip-rap banks that the channel washes into. Any irregularity in the rip-rap, such as a finger extending from the bank or a small slide of rocks, will hold fish. In the summer and fall, current washing into the rip-rap bank stacks the baitfish up, and the combination of rip-rap, food, and current can really attract gold-sided fish.

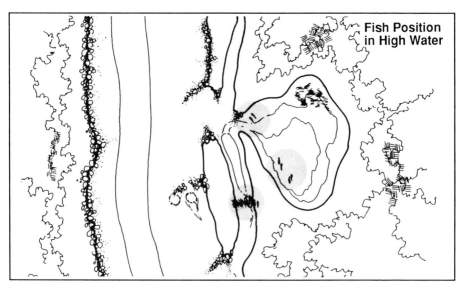

Fish Position
in High Water

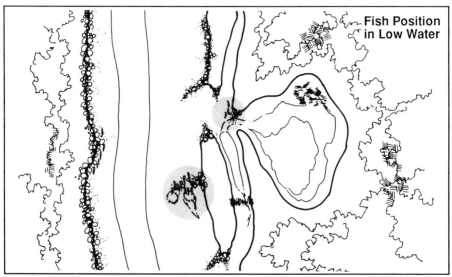

Fish Position
in Low Water

Water levels determine where walleyes will be in relation to the side channel and the surrounding area. During periods of high water, they will move through the side channel into the back water area. When water levels start to fall, they will head out of this area and toward the mid-river structures.

Mid-River Structures

In the spring, fall, and winter, mid-river structures will hold a good percentage of the walleyes. Wash-out holes below dams, sand-bars, humps, slack-water areas below islands, and the channel itself will all hold walleyes. Remember that river fish will hold tight to the bottom, so their position might not always show up on a sonar unit, especially on a rock-strewn bottom, although they will usually be revealed on the sand bars.

In mid-river structures, the most active fish will frequently be on the upstream side of the structure, so that's where we usually start our search. When working a hole, try the lip area on the upstream side of the depression first. If the walleyes are there, you'll know about it quickly. If not, move to the downstream side of the structure. Work other mid-river spots similarly.

Side-Channels

Side-channels are the routes that walleyes use to get into the back water areas off the main channel. Spring is a good time to find the fish using these areas, although they can be found in here in some numbers year'round.

When the water is high, the fish will position themselves where the channel flows into the back water. At this time, water is flowing into the back waters, bringing with it food. During periods of low water, the current is reversed and is flowing from the back water into the main river. Now the walleyes will be where the water moving from the slack water meets the main river channel.

Rocks and wingdams in these side-channels will also hold fish. Keep in mind that the walleyes will position themselves on these rocks and wingdams according to the direction the current is running.

Baits and Techniques for Rivers

River walleyes are usually more aggressive than their counterparts in lakes, which means that at times they are very susceptible to a wide variety of baits. As in most fishing situations though, there are some baits and forms of bait presentation that are more productive than others. Let's talk about the most productive ones.

In our opinion, jigs are the number one, best type of lure to use for river walleyes. Other lures will shine at times, but day-in and day-out, jigs will out-perform all other lure types. Why?? Because they're so darn versatile. Jigs can be cast into shallow water, or vertically jigged in deep holes. We include jigging spoons in the jig category, because although there are some differences in action between a jig and a jigging spoon, we look upon jigging spoons as simply being a flashy jig. They catch fish and are frequently used in the same manner as a jig.

We'll use a variety of jig sizes in rivers. Match the size to the

Jim Beardsley used to pitch baseballs for the Detroit Tigers, now he pitches jigs for walleyes. Jim spent some time on the water with the Pro-Mo's guys and took lots of walleyes on small jigs and light line.

condition. We'll use jigs ranging in weight from 1/16th ounce up to 3/4th's of an ounce. Usually, an 1/8, 1/4, or 3/8 ounce jig will be sufficient. Only when we get to extreme conditions do we go heavier or lighter. Use enough weight to maintain constant contact with the bottom, but not so much that you're constantly snagged.

Jig color can be important. If the fish are active and taking a bait aggressively, they'll take any color you put down there. If they're finicky, try different colors until the best one is discovered. We really like jigs that have some orange, chartreuse, or pink in them, although baits with some minnow or crawfish colors in them have been good also.

When tipping our jigs with live bait, we use minnows and crawlers more than anything else. Minnows are especially good in the cold water periods, with crawlers being better in the summer. Usually, we only use a piece of a crawler on jigs in rivers. A section of the crawler only 2-3 inches long is enough to add some bulk, taste, and smell to the jig, and the walleyes will inhale the whole bait with just a piece of crawler on the jig much more readily than if the whole crawler was used.

Leeches will work, but in current they have a tendency to spin. Give them a shot though in slower moving rivers, especially if the water is clear.

We also like to tip our jigs with a plastic action tail grub at times. If the water is stained or dirty, the action tail seems to attract more fish. When the walleyes are active it isn't necessary to tip the action tail with live bait, but if the fish are sluggish, or if the water is dirty, the addition of a minnow can enhance the lure. For an in-depth look at selecting the proper jig for specific situations, get a copy of our jig book, Pro-Mo's Secrets to Jigging for Walleyes.

Crankbaits are our second choice for walleyes in rivers.

Cranks can be fished quickly, so they allow an angler to cover quite a bit of water in a short time. We'll troll crankbaits along rip-rap, between wingdams, and over humps and bars. They can also be cast over the tops and along the sides of wingdams, and to shallow humps and bars. Crankbaits are versatile fish catchers that often fool the largest walleyes.

Let water clarity and running depth help you in selecting the proper size lure to use. Running depth is especially important. Choose a bait that is bumping bottom, but not constantly getting hung. The fish will be close to the bottom and that's where we want our bait to be. If you can feel the crank ticking bottom on a regular basis, and if you're catching fish, your bait size is probably right.

Also use water clarity as a guide. In dirty water, a larger bodied bait will frequently be better because it will be easier for the fish to see. If you're casting to a sand bar that tops out at five feet and trying to decide which bait to use, a small bodied bait that runs at five feet or a large bodied bait that will also dive to five feet, start with the big bait. If it doesn't produce quickly, go to the smaller lure. If they're equal in productivity, stick with the big bait. It will usually take the bigger fish, especially in the summer and fall.

Color choices are the same for crankbaits as jigs. In dirty water go with the brighter baits: in clear water more natural colors will be better.

One last important concept of fishing rivers is lure presentation. A lure traveling downstream will most of the time be more readily accepted by the fish than a lure traveling upstream. Unless they're swimming downstream, fish in rivers face upstream. That's how they contend with current for one thing, but they also instinctively know that any wounded minnow, crustacean, or insect will be washing downstream. The walleyes can

locate these meals easier if they're facing upstream. That's why, whenever possible, we should allow our baits to move downstream. There are times when this is impractical or impossible, but most of the time a bait moving in a downstream or quartering manner will be most productive.

When fishing a sandbar or structure where snags aren't a problem, cast mostly upstream and let the bait work downstream. If snags are a problem, drop the bait straight over the side of the boat and work it almost straight up and down. Let the current move the boat downstream. This way the bait is still moving downstream. If you feel the boat is moving downstream too fast, use the motor to slow the downstream progress. Either use a bow-mount electric and point the boat upstream, using just enough power to slow the boat's drift, or put the stern facing upstream and put the outboard in reverse, again using just enough power to slow the downstream motion of the boat.

That completes our discussion of finding and catching walleyes in rivers. Rivers, in some areas, are untapped resources for walleyes, as well as smallmouth and largemouth bass, muskies, and, of course, sauger. As good as some rivers are, over-harvesting in some situations can occur. We have no objection to anglers keeping a few fish for supper, but over-bagging and culling smaller dead fish is unacceptable. We've seen this happen below the dams on some rivers, more so than on lakes. Take care of our fish populations now so we can enjoy them tomorrow. With that in mind, let's talk about our final subject, Finding and Catching Walleyes in Reservoirs.

Chapter 10

A Little Like A Lake,
A Little Like A River

In the past couple of decades, the fact that there are lots of walleyes to catch in reservoirs has been made apparent. When the word "reservoir" is mentioned, many of us automatically think of the large, man-made, primarily largemouth bass lakes in the southern states. However, many of the bodies of water in the upper tier of states that are called lakes are actually reservoirs. Many anglers know that walleye factories such as Lake Oahe in South Dakota, Lake Sakakawea in North Dakota, and Lake McConaughy in Nebraska are reservoirs, but, by technical definition, so are Leech and Winnibigoshish lakes in Minnesota, and Petenwell and Castle Rock lakes in Wisconsin. Whether we call them reservoirs, impoundments, lakes, or flowages, these bodies of water can provide some quality

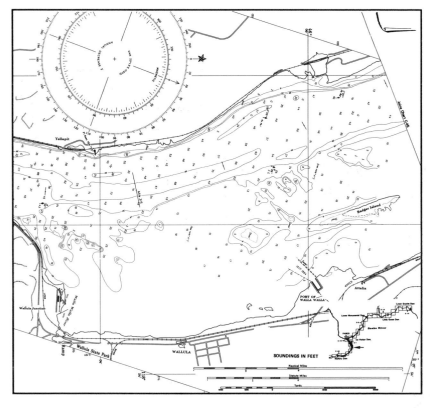

A section of an actual reservoir. Remember, in the spring, the walleyes will be tight to shore and in the sections where there is some current. In the summer they will still be found in the river areas, but will also use the off-shore sunken islands and humps, as well as points.

Reservoir map reproduced from the Evergreen Pacific River Cruising Atlas. Available directly from the Publisher :

EVERGREEN PACIFIC PUBLISHING, a division of ROMAR BOOKS, LTD., by calling toll free 1-800-44 ROMAR.

walleye fishing.

The key to consistent action in a reservoir is to always be aware of exactly where you are on that particular body of water. If you're in the river section, the walleyes will more than likely be acting like river fish. They'll be positioning themselves according to the current and forage. As you get closer to the dam and the section of the reservoir that resembles a lake, the fish will probably be behaving as they would in a lake. Be aware of what's happening in the water around you and you'll put walleyes in the boat.

Generally, the larger the reservoir, the more the walleyes will behave like lake fish. Smaller reservoirs are more affected by water releases at the dam, therefore current is more of a consideration. At times, even in the lake section of the reservoir, the walleyes will be positioning themselves according to a change in the current.

-SPRING-

CURRENT AND CLOSE TO SHORE

Finding walleyes in reservoirs in the spring is, as we've mentioned, a matter of knowing where you are on the impoundment. If you're in the upper section of lake where the river is a factor, the walleyes will be relating to the current and warmer water. In the lower section of the lake, they'll be close to shore. Just as in lakes, some specific areas will draw more fish.

As the walleyes are getting ready to spawn, the current provided by the incoming river or rivers will draw lots of glassy-eyed fish. Expect to find many of these spawners to be on or near gravel and rubble bars that are in water from two to seven feet deep. These structures that are out of the main current flow will be best. Rip-rap, when present, will also see some use by spawn-

ing walleyes. Fish the river section of the reservoir for pre-spawn walleyes just as you would any river and you will catch fish.

When the sun is shining, the walleyes will tuck into the trees. The best way to extract them from the branches and limbs without losing a ton of tackle is with Northland's Weedless Sink'n Jig heads. Tip these with a Power Grub or live bait and flip it into the pockets and holes in the branches. Some baits will still be lost, but not as many as with a traditional jig.

On cloudy days the fish will move toward the edge of the cover and can be very aggressive. Jigs will again be a good way to catch these fish, but a slip-bobber rig will also do a good job. In many reservoirs, flowages, and rivers, brush and trees will hold good numbers of walleyes from time to time. These areas are definitely worth your time.

Rip-rap on the dam will draw lots of pre-spawn walleyes in the lower, lake section of the reservoir. The females move onto the rip-rap, drop their eggs, then slide back into deeper water. The males move in before the females and generally tend to stick around longer. It's a good indicator that the walleyes are entering their summer patterns when you stop catching numbers of smaller males on the rip-rap.

Walleyes will also use shallow shoreline points in the main-lake area for spawning. However, some points will be better than others. Look for the ones that are closest to the main channel. It seems like the fish are much more likely to use these points in the spring. They move from the deeper holding area of the channel, spawn, then move back into the channel. The shorter the distance from the channel to the point, the better. The points nearest the channel will see the most walleye use first. As those points become crowded, the fish will start moving to other points farther from the channel.

One last spot that sees walleye use in the spring is the bays and points on the main lake that have "live" creeks. These creeks bring warmer water into the reservoir, and that attracts walleyes. Although these creeks might dry up in early to mid-summer, they will attract walleyes in the spring. However, if heavy summer or fall rains occur and these creeks start flowing again, the walleyes will be drawn to them, especially in the fall.

-SUMMER-

No major secrets to finding walleyes in the summer in reservoirs. After the spawn, a lot of the fish that spawned in the rivers will pull out and move downstream toward the lake environment, but there will be plenty of fish left to catch in the river. Look for the river to be most productive during adverse weather conditions, and fish it the same as any other river.

The walleyes will move off the shore structures after spawning, and following a recovery period, will begin inhabiting deep points, flats, and sunken islands. They'll be relating heavily to baitfish. Use your sonar to determine which areas the walleyes will be using.

We have noticed that although much of the time the walleyes in the lake section of the reservoir will position themselves according to the sun, wind, and forage as we discussed in the summer chapter of the section on lakes, they can still be affected by current. If the flow of water through the dam is increased, the fish seem to move to the upstream side of the structure that is being worked. Again, sonar use will quickly show when this is happening. Just know that if you're working a spot where the fish were present yesterday and they're not today, and if current flow

Pro-Mo's Team member Tom Brown with a nice walleye taken in a reservoir. Tom found this fish and a bunch more just like it relating to baitfish off a sunken island.

has increased, they could be on the upstream side of the structure. By the same token, if current flow is decreased, they might be on the downstream area of the structure.

-FALL-

Autumn is big walleye time on most reservoirs, like it is on most bodies of water. Expect to find the fish on corners of flats and on the sharper breaking points. The same types of areas that hold gold-sided fish in lakes in the fall will be productive in impoundments. Look for the baitfish and you're going to find walleyes.

There is one structural element available in reservoirs that lakes don't have that produces well in the fall. That's the river channel. In the lower end of most reservoirs, the original river channel is still quite evident. Find the areas where the channel sweeps close to the shore and you've found an area that will hold schools of walleyes in the fall. These fish will move up and down the channel, sometimes moving shallow to feed, but frequently staying in the depths and feeding. At times the walleyes will relate to structure extending from the shore into or near to the channel, but often the fish will just roam up and down the channel. Use sonar to locate them.

The techniques that are used to take walleyes in lakes and rivers are the same ones that will take old marble eyes in reservoirs. Live-bait rigs, jigs, and crankbaits will all work at one time or another.

Although it may seem we've only touched briefly on finding and catching walleyes in reservoirs, the fact is that almost everything that needs to be said has already been said in either the river or lake section of this book. Adapt the lake or river technique to the section of reservoir being fished and you'll be right on the money most of the time.

There you have Pro-Mo's Secrets to Finding and Catching Walleyes. In a book this size, it's impossible to cover all the different places that walleyes can be found in every body of water. We don't have space to talk about suspended walleyes in Lake Erie, or the flat fish on Lake Mille Lacs. However, many of the locational topics we've talked about can be applied to those situations and any other condition you might encounter.

As you've probably noticed, there are no real secrets or special abilities necessary to find walleyes on a regular basis. We can't stress enough the importance of learning how to use and paying attention to your sonar when it comes to finding fish.

Most important of all, keep moving until the fish are found. Remember, you can't catch' em until you find' em. And if you find a bunch of big ones, give the guys at Pro-Mo's a call. Maybe we'll help you catch a few. See you on the water.

FREE ISSUE OFFER

Would you like to catch more fish? Bigger fish? You'll never have to rely on luck again. The world's leading fishing magazine, *In-Fisherman*, shows you exactly how to become a better angler...no matter what species you fish for or where you go.

Discover the tested formula for angling success. Where fish move...how they react. What tackle to choose, how to fish it, and how to use your boat, motor and electronics.

Each colorful issue is loaded with indepth articles... easy-to-read charts and maps... stunning action photography...and much more. With *In-Fisherman*, You'll fish smarter... not harder. Have more fun fishing than ever before. Catch more fish and know why. Send for your FREE issue today.

CUT HERE

YES! Send my FREE issue immediately. If I like *In-Fisherman* Magazine, I will pay just $13.97 for a year's subscription (7 big issues). If it's not for me, I will return the bill marked "cancel" and owe nothing. Whatever I decide, the first issue is mine to keep.

Name _____

Address _____

City _____

State •_____ Zip _____

Save 30% off cover price!

To receive your free issue, fill in name and address and mail to:

In-Fisherman®

P.O. Box 999
Brainerd, MN 56401

Pro-Mo's Secrets

5 Quick Tips For Catching More Walleyes

1. Early in the year, look for most of the walleyes to be near spawning areas. Most of them will be close to shore and near current, if it's available. After the spawn is complete, the fish can be found on off-shore structures, although in some bodies of water they will be relating to shore structures all year. The key after the spawn is finding the food the walleyes are feeding on. If there aren't any baitfish in the area, there will be no walleyes. In the spring, find the spawning area, the rest of the year find the forage.

2. Fish for the biters. You might be sitting on a massive school of walleyes, but they're inactive and difficult to make bite. Look for fish that can be made to strike. It's more productive to work a group of ten fish that will hit than 100 fish that won't. Don't spend a bunch of time working a school of inactive fish, but don't forget about them either. Stop back every now and then during the day because eventually they will turn on.

3. Learn to read your sonar. The importance of understanding what your sonar unit is showing is critical.

4. Do what your sonar tells you to do. If you're using a jig and fishing right on the bottom, and the sonar shows fish suspended three or four feet off the bottom, tie on a live-bait rig with a snell long enough to get a bait up to those walleyes. The jig is right on the bottom, and chances are the fish won't go down for it. Put a bait right in their face though, and you've increased the odds of getting a fish to hit dramatically.

5. Be a versatile angler. Learn how to use all the different lure types and how to fish the various types of waters and eventually you'll be catching more fish on a regular basis.

**For More Information on all of
Pro-Mo's Products,
Send a stamped, self-addressed business size envelope to:**

> ## Pro-Mo's Secrets
> ## Box 686
> ## Sheffield, IA 50475

Notes

Notes

Notes

Notes